Halfway Up The Stairs

Jalaine Halsall

Xanthus Press
• Savannah •

Library of Congress Catalog Number: 97-60528

ISBN: 0-9638295-8-0

Printed in the U.S.A.

Cover Art & Photograph/Gregory Halsall
Charcoal Drawing/Tracey Halsall
Cover Design/Josie Giles

Xanthus Press
309 East Park Lane
Savannah, GA 31401
912-234-5698

Acknowledgements for Published Poems

"Moving On", *Negative Capability* 1984; "A Pencil Box", *Earthwise* 1985; "Four Women", *the minnesota review* 1986; "A Vigil", *Catalyst* 1987; "Chickens", "Surgery 101", *Kansas Quarterly* 1987; "Commencement", *Samisdat* 1987; "The Hunt", *The New York Quarterly* 1988; "Lecture", *The New York Quarterly* 1990; "Him", *Black Warrior Review* 1990; "Swan", *The New York Quarterly* 1991; "Sex", *The Profile* 1993; "Flight", "When I Was A Child", "In The Flesh", *Aurora* 1994; "Frog Of My Heart", *Agnes Scott Writers' Festival* 1994; "Don't Stop", "Liberace's Sister", *Black Warrior Review* 1995.

CONTENTS

ONE

EPILOGUE

Halfway Up The Stairs

"l'estrit de l'escalier"—A French expression, the wit of the staircase: "Thoughts I had going up the staircase that I should've said downstairs." tr. by William Packard.

It occurs to me that poems, in some sense, are those things we didn't say, don't say, couldn't say, didn't know to say, or even how to say, at the bottom of the stairs. And so we say them halfway up, those of us with the ability and desire and yes, the courage, to finally say whatever it is we need to say. To speak, and to risk being heard, finally. So poems—the wit of the staircase—"l'estrit de l'escalier."

Jalaine Halsall

ONE

Nevertheless, give lies the quick dispatch;
Make thy whole vision freely manifested,
And where men feel the itch, there let them scratch!

Paradiso Canto XVII: 127-29

"Without eroticism the mind becomes restless and unsatisfied.
Without virtue (ethics), the conscience goes astray. Without
spirituality, the soul is degraded. Maithuna yoga (sexual
intercourse). . . is an act of profound significance for the
spiritual life and a means of attaining liberation."

Kama Sutra

And when we put completeness on afresh,
All the more gracious shall our person be,
Reclothed in the holy and glorious flesh;

Paradiso Canto XIV: 43-45

Danté, *The Divine Comedy*; tr. by Dorothy L. Sayers; *Paradiso* by
Sayers & Barbara Reynolds

The Complete Kama Sutra; tr. by Alain Danielou

The Hunt

I run out back where the wild grass grows
to fill my straw basket with Mother's hard-boiled
eggs Daddy hid early this morning before I woke
because I still believe in the Easter Bunny.
There's Corey Walker.
I forget he's rough and wild and I jump,
shout, race to meet him, his too-old scowl
checking booty, candied eggs
I am forbidden, my finicky appetite
Daddy says you can hang a hat on my shoulder blades.
We jump, shout, chase through grass tall as myself,
scoop up magic red and purple eggs of jungle
birds. Caught, spun, locked in a vise
Daddy's grip, hand slamming against skin
and tailbone, I've told you, how many times
you can't play with him, you've been told
why don't you mind, please
Daddy, howling, I beg of you, don't Daddy
please Daddy. He knows, he found out
I followed Corey, went with Corey
to the basement where it was dark
and cold and laid down on the floor with my cotton
underpants off, Corey's pants unzipped, squirming
on top, is it in, is it in, feeling
the smooth nudge flop on my stomach,
legs, shouting is it in, is it in
yes, I'm saying yes, yes, he's up, he's running
laughing, throwing rocks, throwing sand in my eyes
I can't see, crying Mama, I want my mama
screaming Mama, I won't go again, please Daddy
I won't do it.

Frog Of My Heart

". . .all a frog wanted was education, and he could do 'most anything. . ."
Mark Twain, *The Notorious Jumping Frog of Calaveras County*

There are so many horny backs and goggle eyes
with squat rumps splayed out here

at the National Museum of African Art. I want
to sweep a brassy handful into my bag and flash

this one's grim stance with nippled skin
that looks hairy and takes me home

in a sunsuit where I waded in the branch
and flopped in a trance, got sand

in my crack and scooped tadpoles into a mason jar
to watch them wiggle. But what a gangbang

last night! PBS flipped me out of that stream
recalled in tranquility. Forty frogs fucked

in what the narrator said was her foam
and his sperm, whipped 3,000 eggs into such spume,

what rapture! Something like the meringue
of a baked Alaska, but I can almost taste

the flavor of cod and mellow out while fishtails
shimmy and melt the glaze, quiver and cling

like slow tears and plop into the pond
as I lean in for a close-up of a cloaca. Later,

lions rip out the belly of a wildebeest and lick
each other's bloody jaws. Never mind who says

what have cats got to do with frogs, or what's the point
of dumping raw meat and screams next to trees

where frogs glide limb to limb like flying
squirrels. I might toss frogs into the grass, spotted

like leopards. Will they get carried away, blowing
in the wind, and rain out of the sky like that old legend,

or bring up Bob Dylan? Maybe you get titillated
by a frog that can make a dog drop dead, then peel

off its own pelt like a toxic T-shirt over its head
and eat it. But this is not a frog

pinned to a board trapped in a lab to be dissected.
And when even a lame cub can grab a bone

and gnaw gristle, who wants to croak
on one high-pitched flute, or even a raspy sax,

for one dull blunder? To both see and hear out of eyes
that are more nearly human! Doesn't that tense

your laterals and make you itch to leap over
a wild bull, straddle creekbeds with flat feet

and sport a wart in the crease of one nostril?
Wouldn't you like to flick your slick tongue

through the liver and hide of a Goliath and suck
out songs like a siren? What would you give to come out,

come out from under that stone where you coddle
your turds like a Midwife Toad as if they

were not merely the first, but all you ever dared
hope to be, or make, of your own creation?

A Pencil Box

It is the first day of First Grade.
I sit beside Jodie.
She has a smooth cap of black
hair and wears a dress with a pinafore,
and slippers don't eat her socks.

She reaches for my pencil box.
Her fingers slide it smoothly open.
Together we examine a sharpener,
an eraser, a twelve-inch ruler, blue
and red and yellow pencils.
Afternoon sun slants across the skin
of my arm and the pencil box
Jodie holds in her hands.

When I Was A Child I Saw Like A Child,
I Thought Like A Child,
I Spoke. . .

I am twelve.
      This is the last year I know how to love dirt
and the only flower bed
     I will ever plant:
               loud blowsy red and yellow zinnias
and two kinds of marigolds, the one I love
to sniff
not much bigger
and blunt like a thumb.
Sunflowers, pink and blue sweet peas,
     but no thin-skinned blotchy wilting petunias.
     And nothing violet-veined with some foreign name like
Clematis
        that can't grow in the bare plot where
my father
     finally got nagged
into taking the fence down
     from around the dog pen
            after her pelvis got cracked
and tossed up in the air by a hit-and-run fender
     and knitted back,
         hookworms sucked her blood,
heaped their plates with her guts.

     I dig with a spade, chop with a hoe,
maybe my father
       plows this little field
     before he gets down to laying by
         the half-acre of corn and beans
     with an old mule

he hires if it doesn't rain on Good Friday.
Everything's inclement, in my new vocabulary,
with him.

I break up clods   **snapdragon**

rake back and forth until the grain is fine

snapdragon

careful not to pack the damp dirt barefoot.
I must've learned *how* from him,
forced to tote buckets from the backyard spigot
to water his tomato plants.
Yet, see
there,
my mother's face
blown-up BIG on a helium balloon
floats over my shoulder
as near as a whisper
how deep and far apart she sows
in straight and narrow furrows.
Ground I gouge
and turn to bury the body

even after Miss Ina Mae Jones nods off, snores
in the middle of a lesson on wiping private
parts from front to back

I am still stumped:

how to know   how to want   to know
what to call
what I found
with   my fingers

after

my father says
the vet said
she's not female,

he's not male, a *Marthadyke*'s

glossy-furred
                    puck-faced cocker spaniel
wagging an amputated stub

                    what pictures
                    form the thoughts
                    make the words

                    ask

what's been disposed of?

Four Women

It was the early 70s, the height of the 60s.
Wearing jeans that rode our hips and showed
our navels, we met at one another's houses,
sat crosslegged on the floor in Yoga positions.
Lights turned low, burning scented candles
while a joint was passed around, we emptied
at least one bottle of cheap red wine
and sang along with Carly Simon. Between us,
we had eleven children, 2.75 each, and were all
still married to our first husbands.

One of us practiced psychology, one worked
for a newspaper, one was a psych major, one
a writer. Two of us campaigned for McGovern,
one was an early demonstrator for Civil Rights
and one lost heart after the assassination
of Bobby Kennedy. Two blondes, a brunette
and a redhead, a Pisces, two Cancers and a Taurus
with two of us on the cusp of Gemini,
we were striking and articulate, had read
The Female Eunuch, subscribed to *Ms.* To the background
of The Moody Blues, one asked, "Why am I not sexy?"

We all started primal scream therapy, talked
about experimenting with open marriage and the first
of us got divorced and went to live with her lover.
Another followed, giving custody to her husband.
There was an abortion and a hysterectomy.
Gloria Steinem came to Atlanta the Saturday
after Maynard Jackson was elected our first black
mayor and one of us marched in the ERA parade
and fell in love with the organizer while another
travelled, sans husband and children, in Germany.

There was another separation and one of us was twice
divorced. Somehow, we all turned forty.

This morning's *Atlanta Constitution* has the news
that romance writers are gathered at the Waverly
while across town at the Hilton, Geraldine Ferraro
opens the National Women's Political Caucus and Steinem's
back in Atlanta. Last night on HBO, I watched Simon
& Garfunkel reunite in Central Park and I pulled out
my old album. All my photographs show us at the beach.

Surgery 101

Your daisies came today.
I resent their ignorant stares
as I lie on this narrow shelf—
cut and stapled—
a thesis some professor gutted.
After a stab of Demerol, I watch
how they grin at me,
yellow and gapped,
the teeth of a prank-playing boy.

Glucose pours from an udder
down one thin teat into a bruised vein.
Nurses shift with sterile eyes.
Poke pellets of glycerine,
scrub me awake at odd hours.
They are rubbing me out.

Veterans parade through the room.
Flash bikini cuts and dazzling
tri-lateral incisions.

I take it back.
The daisies are girls.
Stink like your White Shoulders.

It weighs heavy—this daisy chain
dragged through this women's school.

Flight*

All through high school she'd worn his class
ring wrapped with adhesive
tape to fit her finger, he was the first
to stop and confess her to his priest
after they stretched out together
on the back seat in his family's roomy
Kaiser, their breath fogging the screen
of the windshield at the Scott Drive-In,
the squawky metal speaker
hooking them to dialogue and crescendos.
She could only say that she was innocent
of conclusions, that shadowy convulsing
with her legs wrapped around the rush
from the bathtub's faucet
had nothing to do with his tongue
lashing slippery against the rocks
of her glistening teeth,
his square tough hands smoothing her bare back
and never growing tired
of unhooking her breasts. The first time
her hand slipped under
his elastic sucked-in waist, she slid her fingers
down the length of his thickness,
the capped head spongy as a mushroom,
whirring her desire fast and nearly invisible
as a hummingbird. All that summer
and into the next they drove to the pool
in his new convertible,
and on his first visit back she hovered
over his lap during Thanksgiving break,
his favorite pleated skirt
barely covering her thighs. She sank

down and over him with that slow sucking gasp,
she'd learned to clasp and unclasp him,
and she loved to watch his face
flush as his head fell back, his eyes blank
and wide-open as he groaned. He was still hard
inside her when he told her about the girl
he'd met, that he wouldn't be coming home
for Christmas. Afterwards she couldn't remember
his dwindling, or how her own pleasure
finally freed her to whisper everything he'd wanted,
but only the pinpoint drill
of his pupils, and her panties:
how that first bursting shimmered in the crotch
with quick, bright slashes
like a fingerpainting of her own surrender.

"...a primary mechanism of defense, comparable to an attempt at flight..."
Sigmund Freud, *An Autobiographical Study*

Lecture

"It won't be purged." James Dickey

I look around at the faces
from Ohio and Chicago and Wisconsin,
eager people who want to sharpen the consonants
of the South, so I talk about the rhythm
of everyday speech, especially ours,
how as I grow older I love it more,
and the "do something"
my grandmother said for shit,
I'm happy to say is traceable
to *A Portrait Of The Artist
As A Young Man.* Next I'm on to pitfalls.
It's not good P.R. for Adult Education
Creative Writing workshop folks,
but I'm tending this flock
at a Baptist college that censors F.U.C.K.
like original sin, *fucken*, a German's
fock penetrating something, could be a vagina,
akin to or perhaps
borrowed from *fokken, fook*, dubious
etymology, but *peik*,
peig, a Dutchman striking,
maybe slashing the hymen,
marking his incision like a surgeon,
or a butcher, or *pingere*, a Latin
embroidery, somewhat more friendly by nature
but nonetheless, jabbing cloth
and the skin of a tattoo
by a *gefah*, an enemy who's *faege* or fey,
like Matt Blankenship, a character
in a long, short story, nearly a novella
in my own real life and fated to die.

It's all in the work, I say,
and even then, I go on, doggedly,
it'll make you crazy
sometimes, it'll make you want to cry
if you can. They're squirming
now and know I'm out of line.
Oh, I go high, I go so high. . .
but I'm thinking how all this
reminds me how I never cathart,
and how someone saying *political*
makes me want to lift my arm
and sniff the pit.

Arriving In Hanford

"Perfection is terrible, it cannot have children." Sylvia Plath

Three days and four nights we slept in an upper berth,
she drew the curtains
across my snubbing, my belly tilted and rumbled
through the long dark tube
that screamed around bends and swayed all night.
By day I turned three
and soldiers heading home or slated to go overseas
swung me up
on their shoulders and pressed me in their laps,
a baby sister's damp fingers, someone's little girl
wrinkling sharp-creased pants. "There goes a nigger,"
I said, and the porter went after my mother,
"Teach her some sense." We were out of Georgia,
we were out of the South, on a stopover in Chicago
she dared the wind to slam us down
on a quest for a doll after she'd slapped my face
in the dining car, one woman glared, another nodded grimly.
        A suitcase on the tracks, a dead man
rose out of my sleep in a swirl of steam
that hissed and billowed, my father kissed my mother. She
handed me over in the crook of his arm
like another night's whispering squeezed between them.
Fired from Bell Bomber,
he'd socked a woman's jaw, broke it,
after she'd smacked him, busted his lip. No patience
anywhere in the world after Japs bombed Pearl
Harbor; he got a Top Secret
job with DuPont and headed West. Nine months
in the Project in a 7 x 14 trailer
we had to fold back the bed
to make a table East of the Yakima Valley

where sandstorms whistled
and dust clouds sifted grit between the sheets.
He said he grew suspicious
when birds flew through over smokestacks
and hit the ground. Who knows what follicles wired scalps
and blew out another figment
to fit the picture we were in? Wild new energy
slid down a pole, grabbed his slicker,
slammed on a helmet and rode out at midnight, hanging
onto ladders on bright fire engines—a working man's blaze
like an antidote to the belching
I'd been breathing. Like *that*, I quit puking
and scooped up the alphabet in Campbell's soup,
old fairy tales she got bored reading stacked
under new ones I piled up in bed and read by heart
to him. The sun unshaded everything, dyed skin, streaked
hair like a headband of feathers. "Little Indian" struck up talk
with grown-ups, climbed up and over,
squirmed out from under the compound. Pure icy stream
shot out of the hose less than fifty yards from the Columbia
River; I yelled, *Herbert! Violet!*
and slicked them down under a sky like an amphitheatre. Antics
were a riot, the whole camp
turned out to see them plead, grin.
And still I woke hungry at night.
Blacktop laid out in the desert
crisscrossed in pluses, that last promise
to wait on the steps while they dressed, sidewalks
stretched under my feet at that *very moment*,
too wide, too open, I couldn't stop racing ahead.
        She lay on the sofa in a weak spell,
one arm thrown over her eyes, the other bent
at the waist. They'd sketched out a likeness
to some neighboring kids, what I was wearing,
color of hair—oh yeah, last seen
down by the railroad tracks. She was too torn up

now to see Frank Sinatra
come out from under the stars. I stood looking
at what you've done to your mother, his glaring
away from me riveted to one whole side of her face,
an arm, a leg growing numb by inches. Numbers counted,
the two of them, logic over ethics, some philosophy, a quick
glimpse into something organized
like a union, religion. I was the one watching
without a body; they were never happy when I came back.

Liberace's Sister

Every Saturday Mr. Yeoman tapped his way into
the room, staked out a space, laid his cane
on top of the piano and began to pace across

the gleaming hardwood floor, the heel of one hand
striking his palm like a metronome, his whisper
shaped like a sourmash husk, echoing "Hank and

Jerry's Hideaway" where he stoked the charred
stumps of his classical allusions through the
Steinway and into fingertips, straining past

an octave, tensing for ten. "How quickly you
transpose a diminished 7th!" he said, as we swung
into "Blue Moon." "But I can see. . .and I *can*

see, you know," he added, sweeping shades off his
sockets, milky eyes sunken into the waxed dome
of his face, "how you have to make it hard

when I give you something easy." What could
I say of my diminishing ascension? He sent me
home with nothing but a treble/clef pad.

I sank on the bench at the mahogany console
in the sour sweat of my own composition
while my father blared from his platform

rocker, the full score of Mother's alto hummed
hymns behind my back. Last night I dreamt
I lifted the boxed lip shut like a deaf

mute's over a mirthless grin, and my fingers
cantered across the keyboard as if muscles
flexed bones into music I could almost bear.

Tongues Of The Other

"I will give no other proof than the hawk gives that it's no sparrow!"
William Butler Yeats, "On Baile's Strand"

I bring a handful of songs
with the history of their epigrams
like a mantle of irony that drags a chain
not only of the English,
the German, the Russian, the Spanish, the Bantu,
the French, the Italian, the Polish, the Cherokee
but any language
that someone's bound to call foreign, I bring a chest
so tight that it feels as if my heart
might beat its fright through the humiliation
of a woman who sings what's dredged from a life
in a time when language
always becomes the bludgeon,
communist or fascist, neo-da daist
or deconstructionist Marxist farcist,
pornography or art, I come screaming
with a vise around my skull, my mouth
a caged gate that shuts out everything but a bleat
or a hoarse whisper, the tense tongue
punctures ear drums, pokes out eyes,
stuffs the nose with wads of paper codes
so that I cannot smell, hear, feel, see, taste or talk
around who to quote and who might be offended
and when and if it is wise to say what you mean
and know what you mean to say
when it isn't politic, I come to honor Friedan and Freud
and Women's Suffrage, King and Twain
and African-American Studies, the outrageous Jesus
and Jews and Muslims, agnostics and atheists
and everyone and anyone who knows
what it is to sing in tongues of the other.

A Vigil

*An eleven year-old girl stood trial in Atlanta for the murder of her
mother's common-law husband.*

I come home
from school
sit at the top
of the stairs
listen scared.
Smell his stink
in my hair.

I see his face
teeth spit
on his chin.
Mama's head
spreads red
on the wall.

I vomit
past the rim
dark yellow stains
where he has
missed the hole
again.

I grab the knife
from a drawer
in easy reach.
I run it in
stick it deep.

I sit in court
tell the judge

what I did.
Back home
I breathe
clean air.
He's gone.

Chickens

*Believed to have descended from a wild fowl found in the jungles of
Southeast Asia.*

Milky pink, it lies in my Corning Ware
roaster, plump legs lifted as if for diapering.
Reaching my hand into the gutted center,
pulling out the gizzard, the severed neck, the heart,
I fill the hollow with bread crumbs and sage,
rub butter into the scalded, plucked skin
of a rounded white breast, a thin narrow back.
I picture the missing feathered head,
its comb of red flesh, beady eyes fixed.

Squatting in dirt yards swept clean with brush
brooms, I have studied the scratchings
of chickens, listened to their clucking as they
ate their own and each other's droppings,
black and white paste oozing between pronged claws
yellow and tough as old men's toenails.
I have watched the rising of hackles, the swirling
of dust as frail wings flapped, straining
and lifting and dropping bottom-heavy birds
to the ground.

I am haunted by chickens.
Still running with their heads cut off.

Him

Long after he ran his army trucks
down narrow grooved roads in the sandbox
and pulled out his small gray nub, bucking,
is it in, is it in, leaping, jeering, you hear
his tuneless whistling outside your bedroom
window in the darkest hours of morning
until you can't stay alone,
even in daylight, and stand on the screened porch,
back to the cool stone chimney, a flush
creeping up your neck like a dirty joke
whispered by the boy next door,
peeping through blinds, filching your white
underpants off the line, and the old man
across the street reeking bourbon
as he snatched you away and flipped you
onto the bed, smothering fat fingers
clamped across your mouth, squeezing the swollen
bites of your breasts. One ring, a hang-up, a voice
asks for "Kitty," and a shadow stretches
like a house of mirrors sloping closer
under the streetlight, sneakered feet pound
the sidewalk sliding down your back, a blur
of white thick slugs grab at nothing
between you and him
but your balled fists. Alone in the house
all week you've slept like a child
who willfully forgets, but now at your desk
in the loft, a flash like lightning as headlights
funnel and strobe down the last bend
in the winding gravel drive,
a rack of rollbar halogen beams gliding
like a patrolman killing his engine,
no memory of your blind slide

to the last landing where the twin curves
of your eyeballs train like a telescope
and trace the gauze that shapes
and sways behind the windshield of the scarlet
body, bright shiny enameled, falsely shocking red
as your own blood sucked from the prick
in the soft pad of the thumb, *do you know him,*
know him, you know him as he steps out of the pickup
and raises heavy lids that swirl
you into blank sockets coiling tight
as the stocking cap around his moon-waxed skull.
Like a vague salute spinning cogs,
the slow lift of his hand arcs
and sinks into a wooden tread
across the bridge of the porch,
and you see how his fingers dangle and curl
beside spread legs before he beats on the door,
how he waits for you to slip
down the last flight of stairs
onto the pale kitchen floor shining whitely
across the flagstone foyer as you wheel and bite
into a scream spurting crimson as the rim
of the safety pushed off, the quiet click
of the trigger on the first empty chamber, *think,*
think, the snap-two cock, how nothing can stop him
waiting for the rest of your life.

Welcome To Uppergate Pavilion
for Rosemary Daniell

*"Let me not crave in anxious fear to be saved but hope for the patience
to win my freedom."* Rabindranath Tagore, *Fruit Gathering*

It was no Kubler-Ross induction.
No white light shimmered at the end of a tunnel,
no haloed aunt and neither of my departed grandmothers
held out beckoning hands
with some welcome-to-the-afterlife glow
illuminating their complexions.
Elevator doors opened, the gurney slid
into the refrigerated groin of the operating theater,
and it was like the time my uncle
smudged his face with coal dust,
tied a scarf around his head, wrapped himself
in an old chenille robe
and crept around to the front porch
where I stood, bare feet glued to the blue-painted
boards, eyes skidding to the latch dangling by the door. . . .
      Hooked now as then in particulars, the IV pole
lands by the bed like a stranded stork
trying to deliver me somewhere else,
a steel sow suckling the heart, liver, lungs, kidneys,
as if each organ were a preemie's pulse
growing feeble and indistinct. And even though spirit
didn't slip out of matter and float
to the ceiling where I could look down at the body,
my eyes cross over the bridge of my nose
to watch the changing of the bile,
pumping out of the belly through one nostril
down the tube flowing thick yellow
and dung green in poison code: the third day
burns a deep arterial red,

and I taste the bitter iron in my blood.
         My God, My God, Why Hast Thou Forsaken Me? Christ
pleads out of text while green flies breed maggots on guts
dropping out. Eyes bat open without a blink
after the surgeon's cut eight inches
of gangrene from the small intestine, he says I'll forget
most of his graphic language, but I remember
the purple prose of *Judas, My Brother,* nothing censored
from crucifixion in an old Frank Yerby
novel, gravity's drag on the bowel, I'm cast
like a character stranded in the desert
without so much as a chip of ice and craving nothing
but the mirage of a slushy Coke's head, the Real
Thing would melt on the tongue, alert the salivary
glands, flood the gastric juices and kink the stitched
intestine like a garden hose bursting—
they'd have to open me up again. A call from someone
who says he's Juan and alone in Room 508,
and a slug slides over the sludge
of gums and teeth, hair sleazes across the starched pillowcase,
the night nurse swishes in with a flip
of his wrist, stabs an alternate hip
while hospital security taps the line,
the Atlanta P.D. links peepers and flashers with files
and files of the potentially harmless man.
An octopus from P.R. sways at the foot of the bed
as tentacles drip in, drain out, her bulging head
with its horny pen spews
"nerves, morphine" like poison ink across the official
chart, paralyzing my voice box—they all fling
me back into the unspeakable
role of my mother until a cop arrives with no jurisdiction
over a private institution— Galvanized, finally,
by all my affiliations out of the '60s, '70s, and even, yes,
empowered by Nader's Raiders to sit up and wave
my arms, I'm a *Public* Citizen. Shifts

change, another nurse wanders in while the officer
makes out a case with news of another dope
fiend just down the hall who got a call yesterday. Raw-purpling
throat staples down from the navel
like an old rugged C-section snaking across a faded scar,
and I roll out of bed and stand, green
as the stalk of an Easter Lily.
          Later, I hobble down corridors, sloshing the catheter bag
like a portable pissoir, dreaming myself naked
in the street. I know, I know, there is no lover
who can be the father waving down the hall;
only the obscene caller and the surgeon's hammy, homelike face
shadow me in X ray. Still a crossdresser, disguised
now in a green gown, Soap Sally introduces herself again,
threatens to snatch me up and stuff me
into a croker sack drooping down his back,
to spirit me away to a secret haunt and plunge me
into a bubbling black pot. Yet even as the terror
of my tongue plugs the hole in my mouth, legs wake and walk
toward the old mannish soapmaker; I too relish the elements
of my distilling. Never mind the 99 and 44/100% pure Ivory
bar floating each night in my grimy bathwater,
I was always my mother's boiled and melted flesh,
a homemade greasy lump like leaching lye out of ashes. How *not*
to meet my father's old-maid brother at the unlocked
door to haggle over a spook's identity, flushing
down the toilet of his eyes, even then?

"Soap-Sally"—An African-American fable about an old woman
who kidnaps wicked children and makes them into soap.

Chinese Checkers

It's all in the eyes, the whole story, random and ordinary,
something foreskinned and forepleasured, a game patterned
after *Halma** but more like karma, noted by Plato as well

as Homer, the object in the pock-faced star of triangles
might be a gangbang of four to six or the more ingenuous
couple of a *menage a trois* can play, my baby face studded

with marbles, the blue and yellow gleam already glints
at three, I am the dope, you are the habit I hate
to jump, the hook, an illusion lodged like a glass

orb in the crook of your finger and thunked by your thumb,
and still I am too dumb to move but lose and roll you
under my tongue, hard as my skull, dry as your bone. You

are the father, God! I am the dupe who backslides against
all the rules of common skills as well as analysis,
you must be right, it hasn't done me any good if I can't

transfer out of the bathroom where you drilled my feet
to the floor with the pinpoint of your pupils. Chills,
fever, and the white count climbs, X ray fails to screen

what clenches the gut just under the skin, not a ripple
troubles the playing board of the belly until the surgeon
snakes his hose into the inner tube of my navel, blows me

up and splits the sack, scattering blues streaked
with red; scar tissue knots intestine, a rope
of gangrene cut from the small bowel. Weeks, months,

years later, a globe of proud flesh hides in the
bush, breathes fire like a dragon and smokes
the vanity mirror. O, mien Papa, I came so close

to dying full of shit. I turned into the turd you
threatened to flush down the toilet; a whole battery
of specialists said it was one hell of an operation.

*Greek: Jump

Imagine

My boss swiveled
behind his desk
and said he
couldn't imagine
how he got photographs
through the mail
I wouldn't dream
of even if he showed me
which he would not
subject a nice
girl to acts
I couldn't imagine
being worse
than the book
I took into a stall
at Tucker High School
where tramps
hid out to smoke
while the student body
solved equations
or sat in the auditorium
singing the score
from *South Pacific*
or went on a field trip
to the monastery
in Rockdale County
as brothers
shaved raw halos
around their skulls
I stood over a toilet
bowl and flipped
through photos
of a grown man's peter

spurting cream of wheat
on some slut's titties
so that when my boss
mentioned Great Danes
licking naked women
down on all fours
like bitches in heat
I remembered strays
pawing and humping
my calves
and I could imagine
the pure drool
of a dog.

Go Ahead, I Know You Want To

Just after she told on me
and just after he'd grab me,
I would say to him, I beg of you.
She would stand upright
like the good conduct girl who gets
to be monitor and take down names
when the teacher leaves the room.
She would watch while he would pin
me to his side, an arm
clamped around my ribcage as he swung
one leg over my two legs'
spindly scrabbling like pick-up
sticks forked between his crotch.
His hold on me then was an iron lung
on the blink, no breath to bellow;
I'd go limp, and that would be the signal.
He'd yank down my underpants,
swing one free arm up and back
and slam down an elephant
trunk's low, heavy screaming.
Just before and just after a blow
would land, he'd grunt
and shudder, and I would be dully
counting while her hands hung deadly
white and curious to see how far
she would let him go
before she yelled, Stop,
I'll call the law!
Each time I counted
higher, she waited longer,
I grew older before she yelled, Stop—
Don't you have any stopping sense?
He was waiting too, he couldn't quit

pumping until she screamed
Law or Stop or Sense, and then one
or two extra hard licks might
hit off-mark and change
colors like a chameleon
in the bathtub for days
afterward, I ran a soapy rag
over a blue hand, yellow
fingers and a thumbprint
sealed my thigh. That last time he came
after me, don't say anymore,
she said, you'll make him madder. Go ahead,
I said, I know you want to.
It was almost like a beating, the way
he grunted, shuddered before he stepped
back and turned on her; she'll run you
off now, he muttered. That was all
it took to make me forget
that she was not the one to stop him.

Commencement

I sit in the stands in the quadrangle
waiting for my daughter to graduate. It's 8:30
in the morning, I'm raw, the keynote speaker
droning sonorously, the P.A. system
dropping parts of his speech.
I catch phrases. Reaching back a century
he's invoked the Confederacy,
yoking Georgia to the history of South Africa,
ties with Great Britain, the shared goals
of that country and ours, an unholy
alliance like an arranged marriage
breeding spite and greed. Catchwords drop
from his overfed lips: *Pragmatic. Patriot.*
Bombs explode in the gut of my father
as he leans forward, growling bullshit
under his breath. Standing, balancing
on narrow planks, the Marine Corps
and thirty-three years of General Motors logged
under his belt, he climbs down the bleachers,
the balls of his feet sure and solid
as the hooves of a mountain goat, bladder
puffing like a globefish, toxins
of dulcet tones, misspeaks, disinformation,
the constant shock of pure white hair,
his damaged heart pumping like a piston,
high color rising along the cheekbones
of his Cherokee mother. I turn back
to the ceremony just as the man
moves back from the podium, turns, falls
flat on the makeshift platform,
my father steps to the ground.

Moving On

When Betty wrote *The Feminine Mystique*
I had two babies
wore shoes with spike heels and pointy toes
had forgotten about being
a pistol-packing mama
with my Betsy Wetsy wrapped in a pink blanket
and my Roy Rogers' gun
slung on my hip swinging in the crook
of a Mimosa tree
being Tarzan with my Daisy B.B. rifle shooting
tin cans and targets
while the boy next door shot birds and my cat.
And when Gloria
thought up *Ms.* I still didn't remember
being the fastest
runner on the football team until I was twelve
when Billy Ray beat me.
But when I hit thirty I let my hair grow long
wore low-slung jeans
and glasses like Gloria's so I could be intellectual
and a hippie
and I still didn't remember being a person
without trying
and how I had to work at being a woman
and being a mother
didn't come easy as people lie
and say it does
so I had to dig under Revlon and P.T.A. bulletins
to find my face
smeared on the mirror. Then Betty wrote another book
called *The Second Stage*
just about the time I thought I had everything figured
out with my daughter

striking out on her own and my son cooking
dinner for his girlfriend
and it made me remember my father working overtime
at General Motors
so I could have piano lessons and Tycora sweaters
and my husband
spooning Gerber off drooling chins
on weekends
so I could sleep late and go off alone
and now I think this:
Betty got it right the first time and the second
and I can always see
Gloria's point but I wouldn't want to live alone
and am glad I had babies—
even though it hurts—because everything matters
and I know Billy Ray
didn't really outrun me. I just slowed down
and let him pass.

Man In A Family Cafeteria

The man at the table up front saws his chicken-fried
steak smothered in gravy, forks pole beans and potatoes
and says he's got to put the truck
up on blocks, he's got to do it tonight
while it's still light, it can't wait another day,
tomorrow will be too late, he should've done it
yesterday. He says this too loud, and necks
stiffer than his resist a turn,
but he goes on, truck, light and blocks tonight,
and the two women with him chew straight ahead
not bothering to cut their eyes
to check out who all three of them disgust,
and are not afraid and have not got used
to him so much as they just put up with him
as he persists in his dogged
intention he makes it plain to the dumbest among us
that he's smart enough to catch on to a hardworn
woman's wholesale indifference staring out the window
and suddenly it's not so much
that he's "not all there"
but that he's decided to act downright stupid
seeing as how she can't really be rattled
he has to go on trying, if only in public,
where a whole roomful of strangers can witness
the pleasure of his degradation. Heads drop
over plates, quick looks sneak up from under eyebrows
as seedy shocks zing around the room, the man's
on the verge of breaking down
a plain supper's simple sense
of decorum, he doesn't know how to act, they are all
three putty-faced with grim
reaping lurking behind their dingy eyes, yet who can imagine
the woman he implores even as his common-law mate

much less the strain of their bowed backs on a stained
mattress without sheets? Maybe it's the actual wife
he's addressing who ultimately speaks, and now that he
sees for sure he's got his way, in his own way, finally,
her attention, the decibel level rises steadily
as if he can't afford to lose track of his own momentum,
he blares even louder, smacking between bites.

How Can I Tell You How. . .

The year you graduated, every day the phone rang,
recruiters from the Marines and the Navy,
and when you turned eighteen you were notified
by letter of your obligations, the consequences
of your refusal. And the postman brought Greetings
from the Air Force and the Army, promises of a bright
outstanding future, and I found one you'd torn
in half crumpled in my fist lifted from the worn
round table where an old photograph shows you
pulled up in a high chair with your first cake,
smearing chocolate icing. Can I tell you how
the icicles of my fingers gripped the receiver
the morning after the night you were born,
your great-grandmother calling, saying now you
have a boy, he'll have to go to war? Can I show you
a photograph of a small girl running naked, her arms
flailing limp and flesh sliding off her bones
like molten plastic? Can I tell you how tonight,

on the torch-lit deck, temples are silvering,
and fat lips smack ribeye of rare beast as drops
of rosé and burgundy circle and spread across China?
A stain on democracy, one says, his bald crown
slick as the marinade, a blend of peanuts
and sesame, resistance to sit-ins and hippies,
communists— Can I tell you how he's a whore,
usurping the chant of a boy in Beijing in a hand-
lettered T-shirt, "We Shall Overcome" beats a slow,
steady dirge as memories rise with each
footfall across the white sheet of Forsyth County,
a blanket of snow casts a glare from a hill
to the right, "Nigger go home!" screams deep
into the channel of our silence, ice snapping

Georgia pines from their roots like reports from Jackson,
Kent State out of Ohio, jerking my hands
from the sink, suds tracking to the TV,
popping replays of soldiers shooting students.

The Poet And The Prostitute

Here where we sit around, table the agenda
and size each other up, the poet
passes the red fuzzy heart to the prostitute
who sells carefully chosen words
in whole chunks or by the minute, while I give mine
away to anyone who will listen,
hoping someone will eventually buy
what I say, otherwise, how will I ever know
I am authentically poetic or sexual?
She advertises as a professional,
but I am just as serious about my words,
and my aims—though not identical—are intentional.
We both know and freely claim what we are saying.
Yet she is childlike, and I, in my own way, am innocent.
Cock and fuck and twat strut around the room,
but these words are commonplace
in enlightened circles
and need not mark the speaker a strumpet.
Still, when she mentions a speculum
prying into a vagina, one daughter says, "gross,"
while another squirms out of the infinity
of the here and now
and interrupts the flow of destiny. But a dedicated artist
strives for continuity, particularity, imagery—
I want to gaze deeply into pussy. And I want to show what I know
and synthesize what she is saying
with O'Keeffe's lavender labial splashes
served up in Judy Chicago's hot ceramic dishes
arranged in place settings
spread out on the dinner table, cleared of the cutlery
of botched abortions and the tight stays of emotion.
Tears stream down her cheeks
rarely, whereas I weep copiously at nearly every meeting,

she laces irony with
resonance and modulation and I can see
why men pay her to ad lib
at one and two in the morning. I use the lingo
of the movement: "crosstalk"
is exactly like family. Another daughter
says "dangerous" as mothers
and fathers who became deranged
by comments and questions, slapped our faces,
whipped our asses. Yet, why do we still try to please
like good little girls in pinafores,
lacy socks and patent leather slippers,
who ride butt-naked on the forearms of our fathers?
And I say, what about Euripides
who had to go back to the play and grind Phaedra
down to a woman less aggressively lustful?
After he'd tamed her and brought her back on stage
for Theseus, still horny for Hippolytus, why did she
have to die repentant to satisfy an audience?
More to the point,
though just as broad and generally unanswerable,
what drives the poet and the prostitute
to live alone with big dogs
unlike Diana's, that won't hunt much less kill
the lesser, wilder animals
and I imagine, not terribly unlike nuns
when they were still different, if not stranger,
when they still strolled through streets
cloaked in their habits.

Shelter

Greased brisket of beef reeks and peas sink
in green soup like fat ticks
curdling up my throat as I dole out

fruit cocktail I'm shadowed by an old woman's
hair dyed black and limping wispy as a child's
down her back. . .*can't get them to do anything,*

nothing, nothing, cheap, whores, lesbians.
I won't associate. A mutiny of bottom lips
swell like dumplings in a gravy of sweat.

"Just raise your hands," I say, "we all know
it's hot in here—" *That's right,*
yeah, uh huh rustles like outlaws under plastic

plates. "You have a vote," I add. "This is a democracy."
A quick snap-to, elbows unbend like rifles
cocking, arms slide up waving red, white and blue,

and I'm moved by the majesty and power of words
to march across the room and crank out
creaky windows. Fringed lashes flutter

over the skewed eye of the TV that nobody
but volunteers can adjust the *rules, rules,*
she stews under her breath, *that's why we got rules,*

right up there on the wall and she knows
the rules, MY night to wash,
what's the good in rules when she thinks

she can break—rules are rules. And no men

after 6 p.m., so whose wide shoulders
narrow hips long tall legs cropped hair low-slung

leather-belted slacks and gold chains
gleaming around a thick neck stride toward me. . .
Darlene leaps out of the shadow with the light

behind her face. 2 a.m., not my shift, but I can't sleep
and neither can Mona who still believes in God
though not the pope but likes the idea of Catholics

having to pray through Mary, because men
try to break her down, plots mushrooming
from state to state, F.B.I. plants

in subways and out on the streets, teensy, nearly
invisible sprayguns she can almost see acid
spritzing her blouse and eating holes in her head

nods toward the parking lot where last week's thug
ripped off a battery, spark plugs
from Eileen's cancer-bloated father's Malibu

she drove up from Florida. 5:30 a.m., dip powder
fine as sand and mix with lukewarm water
thin and sticky sweet as breast milk

poured over corn flakes and rice krispies
before the job-hunting filing-away of sleep-ridged
cheeks fogged-breath puff to the MARTA bus. Fish

a soggy dishrag out of the sink as Lenora digs
leftovers out of the refrigerator, stop
to read the hand-lettered sign over the door:

No guests allowed in the kitchen.

Once more, the INSTRUCTIONS:
Take out garbage, check beds, open all windows

in the sleeping area to clear out odors!!
Twist-tie bags dark green and slick as bile
and heave out to the Dempsey Dumpster. Between cots,

take deep whiffs, sniff for something worse
than dead meat and catch a faint scent of powder
like a memory of Ivory flakes and white sheets.

Harlequin Strut

One eyebrow arches high as a coquette's or a villain's
in a film noir as an old lover throws me out and slams
the door. Such camp in the gesture after the old-timey
curtain unfurls majestically across the Plaza's screen,
unveiling more Nazis thrusting Lugers and bayonets
as they strike poses over humped bodies, Jews bleed
the Blue Danube red. In the film, Truth hides
in a music box, and a daughter can't defend
her father. In real life, I'm hurled into one of two
or three dreams, pivotal, I'm told, in the course
of analysis; the knight in full armor swirls
through royal purple grapes in my horn-of-plenty
door and leaps out a jester in booties with long
curly toes. Is this a young Hun, genuflecting,
confessing me with eyes of blue-steeled sin?
Or a straight Arlecchino bridegroom's whopper
about a defective nut that wouldn't let him fuck,
this hurly-burly pell-mell fellow crooks
his finger to lure me back like the closet guy
who couldn't come: all three of Mother's
masks say, swallow, swallow, because I swallowed.
Or is it still my old Pantalone, still,
chasing rats through tall grasses and somersaulting
off his garden tractor, trudging down after the tornado
to argue his point, while Il Capitano, the dog trainer's
attitude of servitude twists the spiked choke
on the collie's neck and scrolls garter belt flicks
behind fluttering lids like a fat horny Buddha
meditating anthropologically and philosophically
on my paling skin with no respect for the shepherd's
whimpering murmur, that leaking aberrant vessel
pouring gallon bloodful buckets into her bursting
heart. . . But am I still a graceful wild

and red and yellow blossom, Columbine
nodding on a slender stem, or the blue and purple
short-spurred petal's nectar bending inward
like a hook? There is no single, ruling metaphor.
Once I sang a clear and piercing falsetto, loose
coppery curls of lyrics winked sequins down my back
in the footlights, my worn and stinky ballerinas
sprayed with Evening in Paris blinked glitter like ground
glass as I swept a yellow ballgown
of cheesecloth across a cardboard hearth and faked
teardrops in ashes for a prince of a boy, charming "Buddy,"
Virgil, new in class, like vigil with a silent
medieval r. The teacher may have pronounced falsely
as she directed the operetta, her Roman nose cut to the
good-looking man who led the band, her horn-rimmed
husband expelled from the ripe-rank musk of her plump-
thighed squat while my rusty secret bloomed scarlet
on white sheets and sprouted multiples of magic nubs,
someone's sweetheart with a white-painted face like a lad
capering with diamonds for patches rises up
and up, out from underground rocks and rootstocks. O come,
come my beloved, if only for this one last pure delirious dance.

TWO

Cunizza, ardent and passionate, had no fewer than four lovers and
two husbands; she speaks to Danté in the heaven of Venus.

One root with him had I, and was by name
  Cunizza; and I glitter here because
  I was o'ermastered by this planet's flame;

Yet gaily I forgive myself the cause
  Of this my lot, for here (though minds of clay
  May think this strange) 'tis gain to me, not loss.

Paradiso Canto IX: 31-36

Halfway Up The Stairs

I'm surprised crossing the Atlantic, so soon overseas
        on an island, racing down roads paced between marsh
and sand where palmettos thrive under gnarled oaks
        that stream Rasputin's mossy beard, Medusa's graying
tresses still wilding on Hilton Head. I've come running
        for three nights, days to cafes and the theatre,
the endless stretch down East 16 cuts through tall pines
        swaying between Macon and Savannah, the speedometer's
needle quivers at eighty, ninety early morning hours
        when our talk breeds nothing so tame as an old friend
hawking "Coffee for Peace" for the Sandinistas,
        you smuggled guns and cocaine in and out of Central
America before an ambush drenched you in blood not
        yours until you rose out of the dead to claim a testicle
for a testicle like an Old Testament prophet. "I enjoyed
        it," you say, as a spurned lover might confess
to his priest, and what sleep you sleep now splits the dawn
        in a graveyard of survivors. That first night you strip
down to a tank top, sling your guitar around your neck,
        the rough-up of your voice smokes the lyrics of your
composition, echoes like an oboe playing "Scotch and Soda,"
        The Kingston Trio, live and in person, and I'm back
with my first love in Georgia Tech's coliseum.
        How could you have guessed that reggae
over folk makes me crave guava jelly? How could I know
        you'd cross an arm behind your head, and I'd long
to crawl into the pit and lick the hollow? I'm in a rush,
        suddenly, to pack and be out of sight, halfway up the stairs,
when the timbre of your voice grips one foot
        in mid-flight, a toe touches down, my hand reaches
for the rail. "Don't go," you say, and I swing in my hot
        childbed of memory, sink to the next riser. You lean
against the wall, stare, look away, need pulling you

out of me out of you out of air, and the mouth trembles
in a pose trying not to pose but to melt what's frozen
        in the flesh; we grope for one word, say, "lust" means "joy"
in German at *The White Hotel.* I drop my head
        in my hands and rock like a cradle as the brainpan tilts,
my fingers rake through the root of my tongue,
        spilling the coiled snails' sticky tracking in the mind,
nothing's ever really lost or forgiven, only suspended,
        and whatever we say past this one stilling moment
can't match our singing as you lunge up the stairs,
        the clean clear phrasing of your shoulders half-blocks
the light and fills the bottom of the well.

Swan

Nipples sting and slide under my nightgown
and I strip it off,
cup my breasts in my hands,
thumbs kneading the stiff ache,
I sink to the floor, one leg
slides under me, a knee lifts, my body
cast in an aureole from the flashlight
I've brought to the closet.
And this from a fantasy
in a bunk bed somewhere in the Village,
and you to the right
of my uplifted shoulder as I stare
into the depths of my own eyes
and begin the slow, circular motion,
the rhythm in the third finger
of my right hand. There are miracles
in these wild dreams,
and my neck stretches long and supple
as I dip it forward to suck
my own tit, nipple
upturning to meet my lips,
breast over my heart
you could take in your mouth
and almost make me come
long before you slide in
I'm ripe as an inland marsh.
Part the glistening lips,
tease the nub, stroking slowly
slipping in and out,
my finger is your cock
and I can have it any way I want
you to plunge and dig
while I sink and clench until your wide-eyed

slit gushes hot and thick down my throat.
My head falls back, arching,
bearing down, panting, climbing
like a slow full yellow moon rising, one more,
just one more blind
toehold in the dark, and I'm up and glazing
over in a mist, lifting
like the morning after
when I can see each bushy clump of evergreen,
boulders jut from the earth
in high relief, and now
as I lean into the mirror
the steady pulsing beat,
the strong tough muscle of my own contractions.

Desert Fling

In the restaurant's booth you reach across the table and tap
my watch. I like that, you say, a man-sized face strapped

around my wrist. I smile as I smiled at the dark-haired little
rich girl who slid my pencil box open, rubbed her fingertips

along the protractor, sunlight slanting across my arm, hot
as your hand wrapped around my hip, that quick-slide yank,

placing me exactly under you. But I'm not thinking of 1st
Grade this minute last night or the watch as a symbol

for the day I flew to meet you and now only hours before I
board another plane for home. I'm not thinking of home,

how like coming home our rocking together, but about hunger,
ravenous and basic, meat loaf, a cheeseburger, the skin

on your face tightening out on the street earlier as if
to squeeze what little time was left. Three days ago

I punched the alarm too gritty early, slid off the bed
and sank crosslegged to the floor, my lips spread fat

shocking scarlet like a baboon's grinning in the dark as I
climbed the stairs to your apartment that same afternoon

the first sight of your belt slung under a goldenrod
shirt, you stood in the doorway cradling a baby blue

trimline against your ear while I reached up to hug you,
my nose grazed your armpit's wires shorting out. And

wasn't I all in black as I spun off like a ghost of Loretta
Young's skirt, twirling past the torso of a dressmaker's

dummy and a fleamarket goddess, one armless, the mannequin
headless, both flaking splotches like liver spots on flesh-

tinted skin. I landed on a Shaker bench cushioned with tiger
stripes like the cheerleader tights I wore in the '50s,

that heart-shaped pasty you'd stuck on Venus' mound kept
slipping off, and I dared to ask about the scruffy deer's

head but never so much as opened my mouth about your two-inch
nicotined nails. I could see how they'd rip out the throat

of an adversary; might they be emblematic of a dislocated
Mandarin whose arcing talons proclaim breeding over power?

There was a war on, do you remember, jeeps and tanks, miring
in the sand. The first missile sheared the heavens the night

before my flight, and I was too strung out over my own junket
to make it to the toilet; I puked over another peculiar American

adventure in the kitchen sink. *Desert Shield, Desert Storm,
Desert. . .* Do we have Reagan to thank for the Movietone

titles, knocking off enemies with remote control, or are we
always posing to kill? Speaking of picture shows, your brother

squinted out of homey slides like Brandon de Wilde, and you
said, why did you say that? Later I thought, ah, he was a cute

boy, and I might just as well be your bonkers mother lording
him all over you again. My eye flicked past a screen of dust

filming an oily blender, a gummy cobweb clung to my fingertips with frail tenacity as I took in the plaster chips littering

the dulled parquet floor from the drilling, chopping-up
of the street below, I saw that you don't clean up for

anyone anymore. Your shoes lined-up on the floor beside
the bed immaculate as conception, the bathtub ringed

with paint, yellow and thick as the yolk of an egg,
twenty-five years chipping off as I leaned into the basin,

stared into the mirror with its permanent glaze like a fog
of mercy and felt merry not having to see my face. Yes,

I did think you could deliver me into some fateful oblivion,
your eyes glittering like jet stones behind horned rims, fierce

and delirious as a midwife's bursting the sack. By the time
our waiter brings your iceberg wedges, a quartered tomato,

a radish rose, you've alluded to Blanche DuBois, and I've
snapped a menu between us: you watching me watching you

watch my every move, waiting for those blank moments when you
regard me as good. You reach across, and I'm a half-beat

off before I see your outstretched hand, my fork balanced
in the palm as if you'd prepared a table before me, suddenly,

I'm far above sandstorms, floating over a thousand miles
to fling my legs around you, I might've lost altitude, a midair

collision plunging into the Atlantic, but who can doubt I'm light
enough to walk on water as I take the fork and begin to eat.

Boy

One thumb hooks his pants
like a cocky grab
at attention,
his drenched T-shirt
sports a hint
of breasts like a plaster
of roundness
that pumps muscles
boxing shoulders
scaffold-like
he stands out
in front and to the right
of his baby sister, weary
of his father's ears,
buoyed by his mother's eyes
and even as his arms wing out
and suspend like half-formed
questions, HOW AM I, HOW
AM I DO — HOW AM I
DOING??? he knows he's the
best they have to offer.
Just before he thinks
of the thumb he forgot
to hide in his other pocket
fingers start to curl
and clutch everything
back with his blunt chin grin
plumping cheeks like pillows,
eyelids puffed full
of the dreams he dreams
when he scrambles into bed
and scrunches his knees
against his chest,

his lips clamp
the salt-sweet stump
of skin and knuckle.

61

Beatrice Speaks

O Danté, look at me. I am Beatrice. The girl
you fell for in the red dress.
And if the light inside my flesh glances off
my hair and shines like a halo around my head,
don't kid yourself. Nine years later
when you pass me by and slide to your knees,
I have no wings to sweep you down the street.
I am lady-faced and hungry as a harlot
to have you skin to skin. *il dolce stil nuovo!*
Ah, yes, at first, I felt flattered
by all that courtly
attention, so many of us get our heads
turned by strolling troubadours, but when you
flaunt another woman, what you say
about "so much love" sounds like *ordure*.
For if this is love in that two-pronged custom
of some long-ago Symposium,
I need a straight translation. And if I
can tunnel backward, I can leap forward:
it's nothing more or less than Rashomon
when Plato says that Aristodemus says
that Pausanius says to bind the sting
of a villain's affection with virtue
and call it "noble error." That's a pretty
speech but smacks of fury.
As I live and breathe, for all you think
and know of Aquinas,
what a waste of a good man to muse
on copulating angels. "It's all straw!" he said
at the end, and that's to his credit,
yet what to make of Boethius?
Lady Philosophy's fifth principle is the crux
of the matter but peters out

and makes another riddle. And so what
if you write my name five-hundred-ten-and-five times
over again so that even I can read
as if I myself were speaking the vulgar tongue,
does it matter? It's all for Fame
and I'm already dead and you in Hell before you die
and you still can't read me, this mute
throne you sit me on, oh, you *are* a Gemini.
You and your swinging lantern,
your head severed and served up on that eunuch's,
Dis's platter, that Great Big Awful Baby
gnawing inside your skull
with your twin soul-mate delusions
and your flighty intellectual illusions,
if I could speak I'd like to remind you
that Christ was no pious pimp. He stopped the stoning
and hung out with Mary Magdalene,
and that's a far more simple and complex matter
than the virgin mother and— God, the fraud
of the holy fathers! Do you think I don't know
in just what manner they are thieves
and what, worst of all,
you stole from me? Amazing how you tossed
the rope girdle down another ditch
and brought up popes dunked head-first
in their holy water douche. Yes, I'm mad,
not glad, and just stricken enough to snatch words
out of Bukowski's mouth, how dare you string words
in mine, and if you took Virgil
out of context, at least he had one. But I!
Here, stuck so high in the clouds
I try to suck in air so thin I cannot breathe.
If I could rip off more than this silly veil,
I'd fling off my cloak and strip all this gossamer
you've wound me in like a mummy,
I'd climb down from this altitude

and hold a press conference naked as a jubilee
down at Chiassi's Pinewood By the Sea
with the azure breeze
twining in all my snaky hair, I'd be interviewed
on the Evening News with Tom Brokaw,
and you'd have to stay up late or get up
with the birds to catch me curled in David Letterman's
grinning gap. But not before the wet sand
oozes between my toes
with the sun beating down on my head, I'll wade
past the rushes and float on my back
and spread my legs and let the ocean flood
in and out, there is nothing so holy
as my nipples puckered and stiff (oh, you didn't think
I knew how to talk like this), they stare
straight out at God, they are God, Danté,
this is Paradise, let me live, let me speak!
Even if I am dead, why can't you keep the faith
in the heaving of your chest?
Unwind the reed girdle and let the blood
bounce and boil back into your balls. Who needs
those silly nymphs chanting like runners-up
around the goody-two-shoes girl-next-door?
I am not the fake who gets voted Queen
and paraded around on a crepe-paper Homecoming float,
my lips, like yours, are scooped and plumped
with dirt. Listen, before you swirl us
off into a River of Light
and tuck me away on some Mystical Petal—
I get vertigo even on Mt. Purgatorio—
let's fool around in the dark
and slide down the wrong side
of the mountaintop while we're both
still only seven-hundred years old,
meet me at the beach. Down here you can catch the tide
as it rushes in, feel the spray on your face

hear the pounding of the surf,
and look, Danté, see how the foam bubbles praise
what some have called your purple phase?
Maybe the similes and the tropes, in places,
were somewhat overwrought, but who can fault
that dear way you faint like Freud,
and you're right to brag and lord it over Ovid:
he can't touch your hermaphrodites
much less your six-legged worm; it's pure grace,
all your best gut hunches. Here, sniff the marsh
and suck the juice from this clam shell
fresh off my fingertips.
Ah, love, I'm as duped, how often I slip
into a trance just listening to you.

Map

Asleep, I am more or less a dream
in the shape of a state, or a whole continent,
foreign country's fat-headed surprise sketched in and
rounded-off, tapering this white shape-shifting shape
like any dreamscape with dark spots scattered all over and
located in site after site and only a moment's memory of doubt
or fear about what I clear until I'm left with nothing but the
empty pale landscape and oh the loss of a single name or place as
the shape shifts and squares, O say can you see how this cloud of
dingy cotton blows up like white noise and fuzzes my sight when
there are no names distinct with definitions puffed-up and suffocating
behind mists of delusions swirling down halls O say can I say
what I see hung up against a door in a brown shape on a green mat
like a barely-formed face-to-face question mark? When I cross the
border with a passport face that blooms full as the moon and pale as a
gardenia curling around a sepia of pink delicious breath, a five-year-
old sits on the sidewalk in front of a Grand Old Home divided into
one of four apartments I live in on Atlanta Avenue at the edge of
Colored Town that splits Ellen from the picture show where she
ushers at Saturday serial matinees, and maids stroll down the broad
blacktop with sacks of tied-up sheets balanced on their heads like the
makeshift wimples of nuns, or plump mortar boards, students of
white women's dirty laundry confessing a never-ending matriculation
as dark-wreathed faces break into white grins, they stop and stoop,
no matter how gnarled their toes, and pat the pale pads of their
fingertips on my red curls, suddenly one leg swings past pop
and hillbilly static, twirling to that last radium dial, Atlanta's
own WAOK, "Ain't that a Shame?" commercial breaks for Royal
Crown Hairdressing, "Maybelline, Maybelline, Why Can't
You Be True?" back to that first spin of "Heartbreak
Hotel" when everyone I knew thought Elvis
was black, I was thirteen, now Rio, background
of blues and splashes of passion pink,

a mall in midtown's sphere of open
latticework intersects at all points
like a giant's ball and jacks like
an architect's trip to another
planet, along the promenade
behind a plate-glass display,
pants and top wide belted and
mossy, hints of a torso, loosed
and hip as the man
at the keyboard of an ebony
grand, jive glossing dark
and rich as a gift of
truffles over women milling

around Friday night's men
at the *al fresco* bar and
track the dream to Botswana
Ghana   Algeria   Angola
Mali   Ethiopia   Uganda
Egypt   the Congo
Zimbabwe   Zaire.

Don't Stop

"Know that the world is a mirror from head to foot." The Garden of
Mystery, Mahmud Shabistari

Last night I thought about the notebooks you fill
in an air-conditioned cafe where you must really love opera
and take your bulging divas back to your bed
and sleep with them between sweat-stiffened sheets.
Ah, the halcyon days when you could tempt me
to strut and strip naked between the pages. How I salivated,
my tongue held in cheek while drool pasted everything
you said to the roof of my mind
like licking those tiny triangular stickers
that hold photographs
fading in Mother's five-and-dime album. No one ever trained
on me with quite that fascination
probing every little thing until you said "I need you, but I need
you strong," as if I had to be molded
for some vital reason. And it seemed right for you
to steam pores and squeeze the rancid oil
from my skull. And I wanted you to prize my arms and legs
open and tried not to think how not to imagine
what you meant about a seventeen year-old nymph's snatch
perched like a surprise
in place of a corduroy zipper. My tongue flipped back
and locked my jaw the first time I saw you
swathed in T-shirts and long-sleeved sweaters,
Vicks VapoRub stashed by your pillow
for reaming the nose and slathering the chest,
exactly like my father's health strategies. You strolled
around in January naked from the waist down,
and I could hardly lift my eyes from your scrotum sac
with its weeping penis
like those early years when he too

pissed in the sink instead of the toilet.
She's looking at me, he griped and glared at my mug
craning from a cot crammed in a corner
to watch him huff by in the mirror's reflection,
one hand cupped over the hem of his undershirt
like a codpiece on a harlequin stripper.
I fell back on my pillow, the dumb duckling
out of a mute swan who only dropped one ripe egg in June
seventeen hours past the summer solstice, I was born
on the cusp of my mother who straddles
my father. Fed up with my infantile
paralysis, ripe to pour all your jism into unraveling
your mother's torture, that night in August,
you said I was nothing
but hot pants and hung up the phone. I rolled over
and dreamed that I stood to the right of my uplifted
shoulder and watched myself slide to the floor
before the waterfall vanity mirror. Stunned by that Art-Deco
revival in my teen-age bedroom, I sat nude and crosslegged
as my neck arched and swooped to reach my upturning nipples.
And I tell you now, that fantasy happened once
and couldn't match the dream's wake like a miracle of evergreen
and summer's blooming reds; leaves on trees
couldn't stop quivering and sighing. Boulders thrust and heaved
out of the ground, and I pulsed
into first grade while the sun streamed across my arm
with a crayon of yellow, a thumb stroked
the varnished mellow wood and slid my pencil box open
to a time for putting away childish things, the perfect
unconscious daughter, I'd met the boy my father said
was no boy, a man, and I yearned, not for his fingers
or mine, but to yield to that searing bursting friction, *yes,*
exactly like waiting for you to set fire through the prism
of your hornrimmed glasses, for him
to rub his thick stick through tough muscle
that left quick bright slashes like a fingerpainting

of my own surrender. *Have I been too tough,* you called
to ask, the timbre of your voice balling my drum,
my mouth watered for the plunge, and I shook for hours
floating in the fume and the flotsam, prizing words open
like an oyster shell. I sat across from my father
at a wharfside restaurant in Florida,
bit down on a pearl, tiny and tinged with gray,
never mind the quality of the thrill
he seized to bully me back to the greasy joint
where the food was cheap,
as if fishing a gem out of rubbery meat
was a sign he'd been given that I could never stop
chewing on meanness. I was more stirred than embarrassed
when you said that I must be starving, too quick to trust
your faith in my gut hunches. One fierce squeeze
of your long muscled fingers
to show how a father's grip makes a manacle
leaves a bracelet of blood around my wrist, and I give you license
to give me hell in the name of. . . What can we call
these uncanny likenesses when we sit down together and talk quietly
and naturally as if you were not tempered by a kick in the heart,
as if I were not waiting for a tongue to lash out and halt.

"How Does Heliotrope Feel,"

you ask, when I'm already on my way out
the door. You always say things
that could be a poem's title,
but when you clap your hand
over your mouth and say, "I shouldn't laugh,
it's just the way I'm made,"
it sounds like a hillbilly lyric,
and we both howl in the middle of how life's
always been with Father. Now he's going to build on
a room and put in a wading pool
and he's going to hire, y'know, Brand,
to bulldoze a tree that's over two-hundred years old
and grade, oh, about fifteen by thirty feet
and then he'll get, y'know, Wert,
to run a long pipe
down behind the house into the woods
where the wild ferns and sweet shrub
and Hearts a' Busting
will root in the Chlorox Swamp
and lure blue jays
and sparrows, a rare cardinal
as well as the lone woodpecker
into the quicksand of God only knows
how many squirrel and raccoon and rabbit broods
will bleach overnight
and sprout two to three extra-waxy
ears that can't hear all the blind
owls breeding bats with pink eyes that hoot
and you say, but that's why we have (your mouth drops
open and you have to look away), GOVERNMENT.
Unlocking the car after the forty-five
minute hour, backing out, driving home,
I decide heliotrope

feels like I'm wearing flesh inside out, sweat
pants bound at the ankles like Aladdin
rubbing the genie out of his blousy trousers,
bleeding scarlet and muscadine
from the waist down, nearly neon and glowing,
but after last night's yelling match
even my legs have to shout bluer
than cobalt and redder than scarlet,
a determination of petals,
blooms that broaden into five-pointed stars
and smell like vanilla, or Narcissus,
which brings up that whole other thing
like being a geodetic instrument: orient the stimulus,
(even if it's a thousand miles away),
strip naked and unfold like a tripod
in a closet, for one brief flaming moment,
shine a flashlight in the mirror;
I am still my father's daughter.

Yes, *Love*, Always A Transference

Oh, these frantic 2 a.m. calls in August
to and from a sweltering apartment in Manhattan,
your open windows wailing distant sirens,
that sweet Georgia voice, you say,
dragging me into quicksand. Oh God,
if I could slink past this ill-bred Electra,
what could I tell you
of a mother who can ford a creekbed
in tarty slingbacks and rise on the other bank
spotless as Jesus and Mary. Yes, I'm sinking,
all anorexics fast and fail
in the earliest darkest hours of morning,
Cinderella hobbling in on one tacky slipper,
Heathcliff keening over my bed,
rattling his death fart. Just before dark I roam
this sulky wood with the collie
and my shepherd, untangle leads, flip fat steaming turds
into vines of honeysuckle and brood
on Grendel's mother. There's no blocking
that nighttrick, showing up with a baton crooked
in an elbow, I pranced down a cobbled street
in tasseled boots, mumbled and missed the beat
as soon as I spied Mother poised
like a green-eyed monitor in a high-rise turret,
I hooked my father's arm, trudged up a close, stuffy tower
and got mired in a bed of priests. The first one
hefted a sterling platter like a Baptist communion,
swapping grape Kool-Aid and oyster crackers,
serving the bride's and groom's severed heads
instead. Horseshit, my father yelled, crass, trying
to warn me, but ah God, humiliating me
as usual. All these years floating
through fog, now some dark third cousin

froths up out of a high tide in deep sleep,
and I'm Prometheus in drag,
still steamy-eyed and stranded
on somebody's glistening rock, your fixation
like a child's infatuation
with Tinker Bell, flirting like a fat-assed fairy,
nothing shocks me out of my horny spin
inside this cedar and glass cock
I've erected on dynamite blasted outcroppings
from Stone Mountain, running underground
on the family compound, scorpions creeping in
all summer long, a Peeping Tom felling oaks
with my father's chainsaw pulled on a stocking cap
and stared in my wide-eyed windows,
drunk enough to think I'm identifying with psychos
who can see right through me. Mother screams, finally,
hopefully not too late
it's not you I hate, it's him,
and points to my father. Ah, at last, the Truth
is, the Truth will out, maybe not in your lifetime or mine,
one analyst reflects. . . The shotgun clicks
off safety, triggers another mechanism,
and the shepherd leaps, her rough tongue eager to slick
somebody up against a sidelight,
there's always murder, you say, in incest.
Not to displace what was shoved between your lips,
but did you ever get a chance to interpret
the first word, shit, out of my mouth on your tongue
at six months is a hell of a synchronicity. Not quite myth
or tragedy, but some variation, say, on commedia carnality,
these long-term projections totemize all the lust.

The Second Landing

Just under a year since the wedding,
less than a week since she moved back
into her old room, and I watch
from the second-floor landing,
his lean, muscled legs pound up and down
the stairs, my God, I think the bridegroom's
finally come for my daughter. The sure swift
dismantling of the bed, everything flying apart,
in less than fifteen minutes, he hefts
the mattress onto his shoulders, the steel
frame like the spine of a thick, new testament,
the dresser drawers neatly stacked and loaded
onto the truck, mini-skirts
and dresses swaying from hangers. . . Yes,
swing her off the balcony like the doctor
grabbed her kicking feet and jerked her out
into the open air
that Sunday morning I was nothing
but raw split-open flesh, temperature soaring,
delirious over her face so quickly
chiseled into memory, our wide-open eyes
stared so hard at each other, I got a glimpse
of something as she boarded a plane
shimmering like a mirage
in the distance. So what to make of his jaw
squared against me, his own mother sidling over
to pinch his ass; did he think I'd help
him bury her in their desert? His face drips
as he lifts and heaves,
working up a man's sweat, teeth clenched
on the long corded tit
wriggling between his lips. Oh, if he
could only bite it off

and suck her ripe fruit nipples
hatched out of my young heat, the strong
sure streaming of all his sticky juices throbbing
into her, he could drench her,
she could cradle him, they could marry today.

"A Kiss Is Still A Kiss"

She folds the screen away from the window and startles a cardinal
out of the Helleri holly, his mate like an old brown sole in hot
pursuit, a promise of snow over juice and toast in the morning

paper, and she stuffs her feet into fleece-lined boots, curls her
toes as if they were cut from ivory, studded with pearls and marble
towers, big toe frosted amethyst, little piggy squeals wee, wee,

wee all the way to market where a man follows her down the aisle
and forgets to buy wine as he watches her fill her basket
with bread and guava jelly, he hopes she won't mind his saying,

she's gorgeous, is she married? Oh, he can't get involved
in *that,* when it's over, it's over, isn't it? She agrees
to meet him in half an hour at one of a chain of hamburger joints

unlike a cafe out of Hopper, maybe Warhol, say, two Campbell's
soup cans propped under a curved glass solarium while rain drums
over their heads, a waterfall slides a sheet over their table.

He steadies his hand around a cup of coffee, he didn't think
she'd show, why did she? Was there really a Cathy in high school
from the late '60s, she thought it was a line, yes, but that gives

him the chance to say he could think up something better. This is
not the first time she's been taken for the Wife of Bath, Piaff,
the Lady of Shalott, Carly Simon. She lost her voice in 6th grade,

Cinderella bleeding into a pad slung between her legs like a saddle
she rode across the stage to meet Prince Charming in an operetta.
Now she's back in school, he respects that, an engineer, mechanical.

Baggy pants, faded jacket; she looks like she's going hunting,

she's a mystery he wants to hold, apart from sex—out of bed.
My God, this woman—what would she look like in a dress? This

may be, she says, my best look, and listen, you think I'm younger—
He doesn't care how old she is, he wants to take her *out*;
he flushes as he holds out his hands, he hopes he won't talk

himself out of a date. She thrills to a word that was hers
in the '50s. He looks like someone too, Beau Bridges, when he
was younger, leaner, some say Richard Gere, he shrugs, slumps,

makes an uncanny guess; she's an only child, spoiled to death
and for all he knows, the biggest bitch in Gwinnett County. *Look*,
he doesn't do *this*. Not as if he hasn't ever. . .in a bar,

but not in a. . .grocery store, he usually winks and wonders what
might've happened. He knows someone as sexual as she (he never
says sexy, and she's impressed by this) couldn't have been all

alone three and a half *years*; all the men, any man he knows
would be wild to wrap her around his neck. She could be crazy
not to think of a gun or a knife, when he walks her to her car,

gets in, but she likes being closed-in with him, doesn't doubt he
isn't married; he's like her husband, always smiling. Can I
kiss you goodbye? *No* shoots from her gut so fast out of her

mouth like an automatic weapon with a kick that snaps her neck,
slams him against the door, and no hint of a yes
hovers between them. Well, at least, he says, I was a gentleman.

Today Poem

I think I feel I need to say I regret
rushing in and giving my opinions
and details about my life
that you couldn't possibly want
to know, I could say that April
is the cruelest month
even though that's merely a reference
to this 18th day of the 4th month
in the 90th year of the 20th century
and you want me to say, if nothing else,
something interesting, when you feel
like picking up and calling Georgia
from New York City, I don't *do* this,
you say, and I'm mostly mute, that damn
long poem. . .all the poems I send you,
I could show restraint
but restraint is everything I hate and your
free-wheeling kicks into me
like one of those addictive
drugs you talk about so incisively,
my own tape played back with facts and data
I learn from you, heady, and smacks
of Pygmalion, always a myth
or a complex about everything we do,
like my two dogs about whom
I remain willfully unconscious
but about you, I see your face
without looking at the photographs,
all your words circling,
but not as if I don't have a thought
of my own, I'd like to pick up and call
Manhattan from Atlanta,
but I'm afraid of holding back

what I'd like to say
beautifully baffled angel, dark slashed
eyebrows sardonically arched, Demon King,
nostrils flaring as if you smell blood,
finally, that isn't yours, pensive, reminds me
of me when I was three, that looking away
from everything into the corners
for something else and that third shot,
as if something isn't paying
off, or not giving you as much
as you'd hoped, your poetry curling me up
to weep, sad lives elegant
quiet elegiac intensity
extraordinary balance imagery deceptively
simple pacing control, your ego won't be
scattered across the floor like so many marbles
ever again, you say, and why does love
turn to homicide, so quickly, and I wish
I knew how to cradle your skull
with its thick springing hair
between my two hands
and touch my lips to that boneplate
on any given day I'm in danger
of being totally unconscious, today
the poem is you.

Sex

You drive by
in your Kaiser
as I walk
to catch a bus
in a sundress
trimmed in lace.

Your tongue is nice.
Not like the thrust
of another's
between my teeth
to make me sick.
You make me sink

"I know you're a nice girl, so you must love me, because you
wouldn't do what you did last night if you didn't love me."

in sweet wet dark
of taste and scent. . .

I am opening my mouth to say how it feels to hold your
nice big one in my hand
when all I know is my cousin's I climbed up behind
on the sliding board
and tickled giggling
under his sunsuit
and you say I must love you and what a nice girl I am
and oh, yes, I am a nice girl
I am a nicer girl
now than I've ever been, I feel nicer now than I've ever felt
and my fingers love your fingers
my tongue loves your tongue

my eyes love your eyes so light blue cotton gray
thick thunder brows slumped shoulders
my mother makes cracks
about, and my ears love the way your pointy ears stick out and
how you say how are you that sounds like who are you?

In The Flesh

I am with you now and for more reasons than one
and for whoever sights and shoots your father
slightly off-center, squatting at the bottom
of the sloping field with the freshly slaughtered deer
pressed against one leg like a child
that's slipped unnoticed and consequently dead
from his lap, the head crooked at a lolling angle
like your never forgotten stillborn brother's
or your bleary eyes that blankly stare
while he grips the ripped-out heart, still steaming
but no longer throbbing,
his wide-open lips grinning so close
to the blunt tip, more like a wedge
than the red, red organ
that you say looks like a brain
clasped, no, cradled in the palm of his hand
and fatter, thicker, but certainly no longer
than a first-trimester fetus,
a crudely hacked-out raw bleeding valentine
aimed at his eager straining mouth
and I see why there is no other
before or after him, yes,
but I won't say it until you do,
how your father with his black-as-soot hair
like the velvety finish on my ebony piano
and only a tinge of gray that might be nothing
but the sun's bright glance off a forelock
is more handsome here than ever, in fact
or in real life, as we say,
with his tanned smooth-as-mushroom brow
something insinuates itself into the slant
of his nose that could never be all-American
but is the dream

for anything hopeless or careless
that wanders across and collapses.
I say yes, yes, look at his stiff new camouflage
and this is ridiculous, of course, one note
of comic sport with his pant legs
spread apart as he crouches on his haunches
like a lover longing for the heart
of the deer, the dead dead deer contrasts in such a vague
likeness to anything radically living,
the one drab animal or vegetable
in this panorama of blazing color
that lies flaccid and unphotogenic in flat surrender
so that we automatically howl to be a child of god
your father so fully in the splendor
of the moment captures the great outdoors,
trees and tall grass under a wild blue yonder
where the surebooted in the big shootout amphitheater
is the consummate stag
in a blow-up bucolic scene of gnawing hunger
for trespassers over the sacred ground of earthly delights,
the great *excelsis gloria* bite, yes,
imagine the heart in his mouth,
how it strings and streams between his teeth
as he chews muscle into mush,
the game sharpens and thickens
in a blood-rush down his throat.

Here's To A Wild Sweetness That Can't Be Tamed

This looks like an assignment for botany,
these blossom-berries I've pinched from the spindly legs
of some tropical vine and arranged, taping them
to linen stationery. Peculiar fruit, probably bitter,
possibly poison, hot pink spongy florets dangling
from supple green wands arced like the spine
of a delicate umbrella, a brighter crimson
than the dusky rose of sweet shrub in May. This past
Spring I almost sent honeysuckle before I thought
how two to three days in an envelope might sour
the nectar. But these fuchsia petals beaded
like an evening purse, moist nubby pouches, one bud
tightly shut and still slightly green
at the center, another bursting pods
like orange pillows fleshing out a bed, and I think
how this one's splayed-out sack, dark
as clotted blood, might tempt you. All Summer
these paths through the woods closed around me steamy
as an incubator under a canopy of shadows,
your voice growing mossy as mulch while I fanned out
like a fern under glass. This third day into Fall
the sun slants a different angle, all your words
clipped back, sentences pruned into proper
English hedges, while this small erect shrubby tree
out of Europe and western Asia blazes
like a burning bush in Georgia, and my voice, you say,
insouciant and vibrant as the Captain
of cheerleaders choreographing kicks
and twirls to "Rock Around the Clock," flashing tiger
tights to the beat of the band, yes—
17 year-old Dingle Priestess performs
tribal fertility rites unconsciously
seeks a life's task, as you say,

the Dingle King, in my Cherokee grandmother's garden,
plucking pom poms off the so-called "Wahoo Bush"*
of Native Americans, unaware of origins,
or the powerfully cathartic essence in the root
bark of "Hearts Abustin' with Love,"*
as mountaineers call these wild Irish
strawberries, late bright blooms firing
flares in the Understory, scarlet as your first
letters, rerooted, and growing savage with surprise.

*Euonymous Americanus

Union

When my father talks about the union,
the gleam of his pupils drill
into a well of memory, starting at $1.14
an hour at the B.O.P. plant
in Doraville, Georgia, January, 1948. Flat
on his back, without lifts,
he changed bumpers and fenders, battery
acid eating into his coveralls,
right side turning blue, he recalls how
they assembled in an open football stadium
to organize Local 10, making up money
for land and a building
for the Union Hall, and I see him
in the kitchen, talk of a 3¢ raise, benefits,
Walter Reuther, Mother pinching off
wet dough, rolling out biscuits fat
as plumped pillows in the palms of her hands,
I see him walk through the door, late,
overtime, much as he can get,
time-and-a-half and double
on holidays and Sundays, I see
the chair he grabs
and twists toward the stove, the way
he crosses one leg over the other,
unlaces black-crusted boots, coughs, a hack
grating deep into his chest, exhaust
fumes rising from the pits, he won't
wade into knee-deep water
to switch on the electrical
system of the engines, get me my committeeman,
no, I can't be a foreman, he's saying, make a man
work harder than he can, while I trace
STRIKE in the milky

steam of windows blocking winter nights
my eyes track his thick, gray-socked
feet as he walks to the white-enameled sink,
turns on the faucet, lifts the Oxydol,
and pours a mound into one palm, working
suds into the blackened grain of his lifeline.

For His Namesake

My head jerks up over the book I fell asleep
clutching, and your skull floats like a helium
balloon cut from its cord, bloats and glows
like a jack o' lantern's taut orange flesh
that buries your eyes in slits, swallows your nose
and mouth in a profile of Hitchcock's pouty cheeks
and looms so real and present
in the room, though you are always absent. Act I,
Scene ii, the *actress,* you muttered about your mother
when you took me home to show off
the diamond on my finger you were buying on time
that I paid for later. It was all a set piece,
no matter what you said you'd been waiting for all your life,
the tongue forks like that freak
of nature; a twin gets sucked into an ovary and grows
like a hairball in puberty. I was brought on to understudy
the mother swept straight off the veranda
of Tara, drawling "Don't you know"
how they'd always loved that boozy dessert, Charlotte, scooped up
with sterling silver spoons out of crystal goblets. Near the end
of the depression era's pink and green
sherbet dishes bought with coupons at filling stations, four
generations slept under one roof in the big house
on Parkway Drive where every night you dreamed the witch
flew in through the stained glass window. By day you stole
into the basement, lit a Camel's red-eye
glow to burn ashy holes in the wings like a gunner's
that sent your cousin's model airplane up
in flames and filched a box of your grandfather's cartridges
to dazzle all the kids with the Lone Ranger's silver
bullets. Stockpiling like a steely romance
after Pearl Harbor, Frank was the first to pull
the trigger on a Sunday morning so soon

after we were married, twenty-five years later the son
repeated the father's ritual blast, suffering from a slight
drinking problem, the wife just home from regular
worship, I don't remember whose head bloodied
a pillow, but I'll never forget your mother up
in my face, whispering her lips pressed against
her father's skin in the coffin, her sickly sweetly
bleeding ulcer, and that wound like a nail puncture
in the pam of your hand from cleaning a .22. And the door
won't close on your grandmother's closet where she
buckled her neck into her son's your father's belt,
and swung from the ceiling. Less than a year
later your grandfather drove off a bridge into a river
somewhere in Florida. They dredged the bottom
and never found the body, but I can still hear
your mother nagging her mother about inheriting
only six place settings of a service for twelve coincidentally
engraved with her initials, she wheeled a cart up
and down the aisles of the brightly lit grocery
store and left a trail of scarlet splotches like a series
of Rorschachs, you might've been Hansel
tagging after Gretel, shaking
out a white handkerchief, once neatly folded. You knelt
and wiped up the permanent rusty tarnish under the fraying
monogrammed napkins draped across covered-dish memories
of your mother flipping into laps and hanging all over
your fraternity brothers, long after the playboy
golfer, your father, teed off in the Society pages of the *Atlanta
Journal;* when he dipped into the till
of his father-in-law's bowling team's petty cash and
spent a drunken night in jail, the news was kept out
of the paper. She divorced him and took you
where the sea washed thousands of shark's teeth
onto the coast of Georgia, your grandfather's government
contract churning out hard cash from the war
effort. You thought it was a lark to climb on the roof

of The King and Prince Hotel like a volunteer spotting
planes, to hang black cloths over windows in the bedroom
where you slept with your mother, wandering into the Marshes
of Glynn, one of your brand new shoes sank
in quicksand. Face down on the desk, blood gushed
out of your nose and pooled on the floor before the teacher
saw that you were not just napping through one
of five, six—who could keep count
of the concussions, you couldn't stop falling upside down
out of trees, breaking the rule
against running after swimming lessons, your feet slid out
from under to beat your brain against the wet-slick
tiles surrounding the pool at the Y while German subs
hovered just barely beneath the shelf off St. Simons
Island, you built sandcastles too close to the ocean
with a Navy flyboy still in training. When the tide swept in,
you took the handsome Ken doll to meet your mother
and didn't know he'd make her a wartime bride before he flew
off to drop bombs in the oil fields
of Romania, he'd make you best man
like a phantom at the wedding and left you nothing
but the groom's gift of a future half-sister. Instead of the sailor
who took you crabbing, he came back a stepfather
and summoned your blood father off the course
of the Piedmont Driving Club, still swinging
his rod in his hand, he propped his foot on the running
board of a '48 Chevrolet and gave his okay to give away
George Llewellyn Hayes, Jr., at ten, you thought you wanted
to adopt another man's name and take your mother's maiden
in the middle, the shortened version of what
you'd always been called sounded the same but looked
so different written without that extra Welsh *l*,
a dyslexia, let's say, of reality's focus
in the imagination's center, your heart like a handstitched
gown sprinkled at a Methodist christening for his namesake
lettered in gold leaf on a small black Bible.

At Long Last

He's stepping into his heavy-treaded traipse
toward brass and steel studs
with bright chrome handles by which six to eight
of the strongest and the only brother left
might possibly lift his body
off the bier and slide it out of the hearse
into a shiny gray vault
cranked and lowered into one of four
Georgia red clay plots,
the only purchase he ever made on time
twenty-five years ago.
One tomb gliding into another,
he will lie in Floral Hills Garden
flanked by an alabaster Virgin
who bows her shawled head in perpetual meekness
on Highway 29 across from Rehobeth Baptist,
this week's marquee announcing
what God has to say about homosexuals.
My father's vision of a future
where he is not present
will pay off for me, I won't have to dip
into savings or get a loan,
he's always provided cash to ease transitions
and in this present one he is eager
to use the shotgun he bought with his first paycheck
from Sears-Roebuck when he was seventeen.
"Bullshit!" he says, and slings a fist
whistling past the tip of my nose
as it thuds into his calloused
palm, he swears he will ask God
Almighty to take him to a Better Place
or swallow Percocet with a pint of liquor. A buddy
at Parris Island got blown to smithereens

after he was sent overseas,
but last night he stood at the foot of my father's bed:
I was awake, he says, it was no dream.
Seventy-five years ago his bullet head shot
out from between my four foot-ten grandmother's legs
and the colicky sobbing made her swaddle
and tie him in a sling down her back while she stirred
boiling clothes and fed wood to a pot-bellied fire
and not even my mother's coming-unglued
querulous bickering can match his lust for life smashed
inside his Model-A hit-and-run drunken
father's bits of skull and sticky wrinkled matter
splattered across Highway 29, all the accidental
nights he's yearned to scotch the shotgun against his knees,
jam the barrel between his teeth and bite back
into one never-ending scream.

Cradle The Rapture*

"It's the feast of the Goddess, we've nothing to fear." Aristophanes, *The Frogs*.

1.

Strange, you say, to be riding in the car with someone who
doesn't know her way around the island, and I know I'm not the one
you murmured over, rushing the receiver into the kitchen,
the sight of my breathing makes you stare livid across the corn
chowder. Odd, too, how you took me to task over Shallowford
Road, too-traveled and close to home to tear the word apart,
yet look, because of you, less than two weeks later I can't stop
thinking in symbols as I ford the shallow stream beside your
townhouse, the heel of one boot sinks slightly backward into
     the quicksand of all my nightmares
     when I couldn't stop following Mother.

2.

Climbing the bank on the other side, I'm a witness, suddenly,
who can't stop analyzing how all this actually happens. Maybe
the Spanish moss that drapes the trees blinded her and lures me
straight to the spot where the cardinal's lying. No ants swarming
in and out of her feathers, no stink, no hint of foul play, and no
hollow rounded breast collapses when I prod the limp body, close-up,
even dead, she's rose-beige; one swift dip in a pot of vermilion
stains her bill and wingtips and stings the eyes as she streaks
the sky at full tilt in hot pursuit
     of her scarlet lover, she's olive
     drab, drained of all his color.

3.

At the gift shop you're already at the checkout counter with yet
another of your Madonnas clutched in your fist when I'm tempted

by a glass frog, you say, I should buy her a present, don't you
think? What skinny tall wooden half-man, half-rabbit does she
collect, bowing her head too close to his in public, she probably
craves a dozen or more like him, that's why she read your journal.
But she's my *wife*, you drop your head in your hands, and I'm
stricken stupid and mute in my own behalf over her leaving you
after you balled the one you'd lusted after a year and a half
even before I knew you, you'd married this last one so white she
might as well be Mother; the innocent always eat what's inside out
of us. We've unleashed the Furies,
          the Harpy, and the masked shrew
          aches to bury all three of us.

                              4.

I can't stop seeing the songbird hurtling into the old live oak
she was lying under, a vague slight twist to the angle; she'll risk
her neck in the flash of her soul's twin brother. The cardinal's
first in the Zodiac, a vine, a vein, a vowel, the wind, a flower,
a ship, a number, seven sins for seven virtues, her sun's in Cancer
on the cusp of the moon in Gemini, both hatched in June out of Leda
out of the Swan, he's a double star in that same constellation, she's
the first, the only one who's asked him to sing when they meet
in December at the equinox on an island off the coast of South
Carolina, trees light the sky in a festival of sparklers, *O Holy
Night!* Scorpio rises, and the redbird's caught like a slave,
a feather in a woman's hat, the original St. Nicholas who carols her
body on Christmas Eve, he tosses his emperor's cap into the air
of Heaven while a bewitched child stumbles across
a bloodless murder: eight inches of dead bird measures
the gangrenous cord cut from my vitals,
Mother still coiled in the cavity as I blot everything
from the main channel for hours, years, maybe forever, walk away
from the cardinal's knowledge with maggots gnawing
          to eat pizza, watch "Shadows
          and Fog," a Blockbuster movie.

5.

All my nerve endings arc like a rainbow of bruises blotching her
cheeks when you kiss her less than a foot from my face, I'm sunk
in this sit-up-and-die solution until the two of you swing out
the door as if Noel Coward wrote the role of the husband especially
for *mon petite*. I'm a stranger I can never imagine, so raptly
abandoned in willing humiliation, out of wedlock, illegitimate,
leaving and leaving last night, so strung-out at two in the morning
I staggered back. Can you hear how my packing drums up and down
the stairwell, cymbals crash, echoes whistle and shriek under
blankets and sheets as I grab a stray sock, do this, do that,
and the pen snatched at random spills ink too absurdly crimson
keening across the note I'm leaving you some swipe at civility
to staunch the bloodstew boiling out of my bowels. An ungodly
scream strips skin off black-festered highways, a Mermaid splits
a fin and kicks her way out of the proud flesh of my belly, howls
at a hundred miles an hour north to Atlanta, I'm mad to straddle
the Mark VII like a seahorse sawing through oceans of rainwater,
brand new wipers slash the windshield that can't stop streaming, one
lens popped out of my wire-framed glasses, possibly still lost
in the toe of her dusty high-heeled shoe, a black cherry bra
like a siren's lipstick smeared across your shag carpet, the other
wandering eye's skewed prescription pivots Mother onto Daddy's
shoulders; her legs ring a horseshoe around his neck in a snapshot
of that record snow in 1940, the year they got married before
I was born in Georgia, the three of us hang
        from the drenched sky in one
        raindrop's shimmering bubble.

6.

I agree it doesn't matter whether your wife and her jackrabbit
did the deed, I don't give a fat bunny's ass about humping bunnies
either, I'm haunted by chickens still running with their heads cut
off, and I need to speak rampantly before mine's severed. . . Listen

to the Frogswans hit the cleanest, sweetest notes in the purest
harmony of tone, and rock to another beat altogether, say, reggae
blows Pan's pipe in Symphony Hall when a man hugs a cello
between his thighs in his hands and plucks his own strings
like hymns out of "Graceland," no wonder Charon
ferries us home over the bog of all our sticky streaming juices,
Agape makes me crazy to cream a goat, invoke Reich,
all the word salad in *Savage Sleep*, the French can't *like*
anybody, in Paris it's all Eros in the *Kama Sutra* fucking's
Maithuna yoga and Hell's Heaven scraping your square jaw's
two-day stubble
        in the palm of my hand, razor-burn
        on my chin croons its own torch song. . .

even as

7.

Time declares Freud's libido dead in America, I squat beside perfectly
tucked wings, tiny clawed feet crossed at the ankles, rouge around
the ruff of my breast as if skating on air, I'd spun in mid-flight
while one swirling instant's magical brush tints the fringe, one last
fierce crawl through the ashes of grey-out aphasia, finally deliri-
ously naked, body over body, my tongue wraps around yours, and
I'm wild to slide under the light brown bird, cradle the rapture, lay
her at your feet and crouch on your chest, frog on my heart in my
mind on my lips, I love how you say, I love
        how you start to dance
        the minute I touch you.

"Birds were companions for games. . .attributed with great intel-
ligence. They carried ardent messages between lovers, and during
war, secret instructions." *The Complete Kama Sutra*

Savage Sleep, Brand, Milton.

Bang The Walls Gently

"He prayeth well, who loveth well / Both man and bird and beast."
Samuel Taylor Coleridge

Last night when you agreed to caretake my parents' house, to move
    in and take my father's bedroom for your own, I sank
to the floor over the hypodermic I'd found hidden
    in his medicine cabinet and remembered how your voice
hovered over two tickets to the symphony, hopeful I'd turn
    down a Saturday concert so late in the morning of the same
afternoon. But I love the cello, I said, and you'd think by now I'd
    know the masculine pitch, that hoarse lowing of the "young
man's heart's complaint." I did think, instantly, of the cardinal who
    woke me that past Monday and drummed on my window
loud as a woodpecker as he cruised the bedroom wing for
    seven weeks and hung in a swirl of feathers like a scarlet
hummingbird, mad to suck me out through glass. I need no
    bird-code spectacle on the grief in passion
after nursing Noah through two five-hour surgeries three weeks
    apart, I need your face unexpectedly present when I recount
how he slid across the leather seat paralyzed to the neck,
    his asshole flaccid, soiled blankets and towels left behind
in the car after the race to the hospital; yea, though I drive
    through the valley of the shadow and get my first speeding
ticket in Barrow County, my dog's shit comforts me on the way home
    in the dark like an orchard too ripe to harvest, dogwoods
in full bloom four days before Good Friday blaze an afterlife
    where god *is* dog, and my dog's blood soaks through
the cardboard casket too small for a collie shepherd, unwieldy
    as I drive into the field, shift the Lincoln from ambulance
to hearse into Park, train the headlights on the gravediggers,
    while we bury Noah in my father's garden, he mixes codeine
with morphine and Tennessee bourbon, Toradol, Tylox, Mellaril,
    Methadone, and Xanax for my mother, Lortab, Demerol,

Darvocet—My father stages an exit, leukemia masks the killer
     and drains the body so fast as to mystify the doctors: skin
swings slack on his arms in less than two weeks. I sit beside him
     at Piedmont Hospital, watch the drip into a vein
where he lies for long hours and contemplates the blood of strangers,
     his own blood kin, his only child, my divorce he never meant
to happen lights a torch under my mother's tailbone,
     when she takes to her bed for three years to head off
my father's Emergency Room enemas, no number of magnetic
     resonating imagings, myelograms, CAT scans locate the
tumor that floats out of his brain into her groin. And you, with your
     odd timing after all the acting lessons, stepping so boldly
into my life of bodily excretions, transfusing one
     element into another, air filled with smoke, the scent of
fireworks or metal burning, a .38 lying on the floor next to my
     father's hand so cold his arm slips loose and rubbery from
my grip after 911 directs me back to take a pulse, I have to step over
     him and the gun to get to my mother, lying in her brass bed
with four gleaming posters, her face wiped pale in pink pajamas,
     a blanket tucked under her arms he must've crossed over her
breast like Sleeping Beauty waits for her prince sprawled
     barefoot on the floor in a dingy T-shirt, his head slung back,
his face gnarled into lumps like glue and tinted with ashes, his mouth
     gapes over what his left hand helped his right to pull the
trigger of the silver pistol, a cowboy's quick draw out of a holster.
     I knew so long ago before I forgot I must always remember
the least my father would do if he could no longer bang her was
     shoot her, the hole in his heart so deep if not so black with
soot you could see all the way through them, some seepage like
     castor oil or semen circles identical twin wounds
tiny as the vaginas of violated virgins, I have shrunk my skull in this
     tunnel of their last consensual coupling, no little convulsing
into ecstasy that will not do us part, no carving his hip
     from her spine. After the funeral director opens the lids,
I pace between matching walnut caskets draped with blankets
     of stargazers and snapdragons, my father so lean

in the coffin, so much like a lover who strolled off
      with my song still strung in his guitar, a Gemini
like my mother, and like Noah, who means *rest* in Hebrew, she sang
      alto to my soprano accompanied by my piano, while my
father played the banjo by ear; it seems we've all been practicing
      these stringed instruments so vital to the art of lovemaking,
this is my grim Electra, I have no shame as I lean over her, call him,
      my love. When a gun fires twice, lingers and reports
at 3 a.m. over a week later, I know no reason why my father's
      blood dried stiff on the carpet comes up wet on my fingers,
or why the cardinal on the morning of the funeral swoops one last
      frenzy and chants the bliss of rapture like a red-winged
prophet at the altar of his beloved out on a limb beside him
      I slide dresses and blouses along a rod in the closet, a salmon
skirt scatters white daisies, buttons down one side and kicks
      a front pleat as I walk out to meet you intent on something
not entirely your own making the slight squint, you say
      you don't know why you need me, I joke about melting
in the heat of late May, neither of us prepared to sit so close
      to the orchestra and dissolve in the salty sweat drops
flying from the cellist's lit face as he grunts and tosses his head
      like a Lippizaner's hugged between thighs of his own gruff
murmurings, some movement subtle as dressage strums blue-white
      notes that sparkle hot tears when the cello's husky voice
whispers airs above the ground, let no man cast asunder one day
      sunlit and plucked out of the Father's eye cocked like a
Cyclop's stabbing icicles from Hell as you carry my new shoes
      with a husband's grace through underground parking at
Phipps Plaza, I have to think clearly, who played the lead,
      the ease of your performance when you starred as *The Toyer*,
not long after you went to bed every night sticky from your mother.
      I'm on the verge of so much yet to unravel,
my key poised for the lock, I have only to turn the knob and step
      across the threshold into the stillness of the kitchen,
lay their mail on the darkly gleaming island with wheat bread and
      bananas ripening before I call "hello?"

into the hollow of my life like a lady in waiting for the worst
     I'm still pretending hasn't happened as my feet slap the floor
muffled onto carpet in the dusk of the hall, one foot shifts away
     from a pink chiffon dress and a gray suit already laid out
on his bed, two envelopes taped to the TV I never see as I swerve and
     veer past her lingerie chest so delicately, gently curved,
blushing peach under blue sanded down to bare wood and skimmed
     with white, my breath caught in my throat like a funnel
sucking death, this is the room of my conception three months
     after a back-alley abortion in June, 1940, if not for that first clot
dropped in a slop jar, I wouldn't have been born in June a year later,
     six months before Pearl Harbor. I wouldn't have traveled
with my mother four days and three nights like strangers on a train
     to meet my father on the Hanford Project before he joined
the Marines, four years I kept him out of the war to end all wars as
     my tongue trolls the gluttony minute to hour, days and weeks
dip into the bloodspill months later in the Valley of Peace
     at Floral Hills Garden, my father still dogs me with his
story as I crouch in new grass, a pink and magenta silk bouquet
     I've arranged as my eyes water over a splotch the shade
of my father's on the carpet that stains the marker embellished
     with roses too soon for rust engraved around their names
"Together Forever." This is the bed of my making, and my mother
     lies in it named the victim in the police report eternally
innocent, and I, the complainant, the only witness, not long by either
     of their sides, my father the suspect, lost in the wood
of the suicides with powder burns on his fingers
     stretches on the floor with the gun between them.

I Lived In Trees

*For Athena, dubbed "Goddess of Wisdom" in 1959 by her husband's
fraternity at Georgia Tech, the Pikes, as if they foretold that moment
twelve years later when he signed her into the locked ward at Peach-
ford at which time she observed: "We have to go back to the jungle."*

Eyes trapped behind bars like a raccoon's stare out of sockets
ringed with bruises, and I imagine Athena even more acutely now
since my father shot himself in the heart after he shot my mother
in the heart as I hang halfway upside-down in a dogwood
choked in vines, one foot scotched in the crook of a limb, legs
stretch into a split, one last lunge skyward, and the lopper
I've dragged up the trunk gnaws the thick chewy rope,
yanks the coarse-leafed kudzu laced with the sweet venom
of honeysuckle, muscles of muscadine braided with greenbrier
like dreadlocks that slither past and hit the ground with the stealth
and weight of boa constrictors. Limbs quiver while tender
scalloped leaves flutter free as my life as a child,
scaling heights as I swung by my feet from the boughs of Mimosas
and picked their pink-stringed blossoms
to make applesauce for my family of dolls, Susan, Pamela, Wanda,
all during that time between eight and twelve when I lived
in trees. I kiss this tree's living bark as I kissed Noah,
my collie shepherd's widow's peak just above his eyes, now dead
too and buried in my father's garden less than thirty yards
from where I weep through sweat and dust streaking my face
with no one to see and everything green and growing spread out
before me, these weeks stretch into months, and sometimes I pee
outside with a small bold relief, and then back hacking vines
out of hell, and from Japan, off pines and oaks, hickorys,
maples, farmland gone to forest, still sweeping from the crown
of the hill like a ballgown, long terraces heaped with stones
like jewels, fields my father plowed as a boy. "Work is holy,"
a friend says, his output suddenly voluminous. Yes,

I'm "working the land," reclaiming it, *Paradise Regained*
after Milton's Satan meets his intellectual equal in Eve,
Adam strips down to the trembling earth where wild ferns
fan into feathery beds down by the creek, in the darkest shadows,
Euonymous Americanus, "Hearts 'a Busting with Love," sleek
umbrella-vined tree arcs heavy with hot pink fruit, blooms
ready to burst orange berries—this work
that scars my hands, cracks my nails, and makes the fingers
of my right hand short circuit, tiny shocks from the squeezed nerve
in the wrist's carpal tunnel, arms and legs clawed and gashed,
my whole body stiff and blotched with blood as if I'd pitched
headfirst into the Understory to fight the feral cats
rather than feed them, or run blindly to meet the many-antlered buck
who ruts against my bedroom window in the Fall, setting off
the AT&T Quantum alarm, helicopters flying low,
floodlights flashing like heat lightning while the Gwinnett County
police, guns in holsters, thrash through the bush at midnight.
Even the pine beetle requires whole trees, sometimes two at a time
house randy males lured by one female's love scent as they suck
the sap from the Cherokee's sacred pine until all the bark flakes off,
chunks of scabs, an exzema, say, of a fatal STD picked up
in the Red Light District of Insects, exposing smooth yellow
flesh of trunks, naked and long since dead. This is nature,
the arborist scolds, despite hundreds of hours scowling
in deep study for two degrees beside his name on a card,
as if any attempt, his or mine, to bring order in the face
of fucking and dying. . . Each night I step from a shower
scrubbed of the loam and game of wood's dirt, wrapped in a white
terry cloth robe, fresh as a newborn and warm as a glass
of milk drugged for sleep: every muscle and joint strains and aches,
hot chills ripple like tiny fingers across my skin, a delirium
of weariness earned with sweat and blood so oddly blue,
almost purple, pale yellow eggs scrambled in butter, asparagus,
melons and tomatoes, my own sweetened
tea with a twist of lemon down my throat, and I know nothing
of this stand of trees I've sworn to free from the clutch

of vines, taut wires that snap off whole tops,
vines intertwined in disguise, a masquerade of papery leaves
that coil on the ground limp and gauzy as G-strings
after I've stripped them from gored trunks
deceptively light as they creep forward, reach for a branch,
spiral up and around in a vise like a web, an internet of vines,
silent and nearly invisible, ordinary as neighbors. Ah yes, Nature.
Any dew-eyed morning's sun dapples through a canopy of leaves
with some unique design, like a fine-woven tapestry, so quiet
and cool, so unexpected, these isolated clearings, as I happen
onto the pine-needled floor of a glade I know only
that this is no garden I choose to come home to this rocky, rolling
land my father left me growing tangled, knotted at the roots.

This Truck

I climb into the cab of the International with the key that, yes,
thankfully, blessedly, fits, turns the ignition, a key that somehow,
through all these months almost a year since my father
shot my mother and himself, I've managed not to lose, and I am moved
beyond the moment, even though no motor roars to life,
by my own good sense or luck not to have lost the key, to have hung
it on the wall safe beside all the others,
and suddenly happy as a child might be happy
who's climbed into her father's truck to sit on his lap
and grip the huge steering wheel with her small hands guided
by his driving down a dirt road. . . This scene may have happened,
I don't exactly remember, I only know I want this truck
that I cannot drive, whose clutch takes the heavy boot of a man,
I need my father's truck to work these fourteen acres
he's left me. "What are you making?" someone wants to know,
and I say I'm freeing the trees. Vines: honeysuckle, muscadine
and greenbrier, all braided together with the dreadful
kudzu from Japan, whose smothering presence all over the South
must be an entire nation's penance for Nagasaki, Hiroshima,
and mild punishment, at that, yes, pitted against scorched earth
and decades of blasted genes, our landscape gulped down
the throat of the Jade Dragon slithering across Georgia,
swallowing tall pines and whole billboards, not since Sherman,
have we been so overrun, yet, *mea culpa, mea culpa*. For now,
to be inside the International is to be filled with goodwill,
my father's truck that he bought from Cofer Bros. in 1970 acts
as a tonic to health and reason, they don't make trucks
like this anymore, nearly extinct as the wildebeest,
and my father with a 4th grade education
who worked at General Motors, who'd made a small fortune
in real estate but still wore his Sears Roebuck and Belk Gallant
coveralls and sat laboriously patching all the grease-stained
pairs that my mother refused to mend anymore since by that time

he could've bought a closetful of coveralls, a fleet of trucks,
bright shiny new, lightweight and plastic, all of them together
not worth the International's manifold. I don't actually know
what a manifold is, but here is the choke, the gas pedal,
the brake and the curved gear shift with its dark
round knob where I sit on an old bright yellow scatter rug
that covers the torn upholstery, one that my mother
threw out and he recycled before it was politically correct,
which drove her crazy, the red body dulled by rain and ice,
heat, scraped and dented having rambled over rock-strewn fields
and bucked between trees draped in kudzu that he dug up
and ripped out of the ground by its roots, 22 point something
nearly 23 acres before selling off eight across the creek
which he forded in this working truck, as "Carrot,"
from Buice Body Shop, who sent a spray to the funeral,
says, that's no riding truck when I ask him if it's a classic:
"Worth a thousand dollars." Everything I don't need
and can't keep, I've given to the one brother and four
sisters between them, my aunts and uncles, except for the 1980
Cadillac I sold for $3,000, but the new Lincoln Townhouse
with only about 12 miles on it that was my mother's last new
car that she never drove I sold to an Indian couple
who placed three lemons and one coconut under each tire,
the coconut being the sacred fruit of the Hindus
and coincidentally a favorite, fine snowflakes
my father grated that my mother stirred into the coconut milk
along with cow's milk and sugar, the filling that soaked
between layers of her 1, 2, 3, 4 egg
and butter Christmas cake, and my father's lust for lemons,
a whole bowlful of wedges he squeezed, making lemonade,
my mother said, out of her sweetened ice tea
but now one hard, hairy shell
like a monkey's skull the wife places under the Lincoln's
right front tire along with the three lemons (which inclusion
in the ceremony may derive from Western influence)
while the husband shrugs, announces he is not religious

but humors his wife, driving over explosions
of crunches and squishings, after which she gathers
the smashed fruit in a Glad sandwich bag for tossing
into the lake behind their house, the final, necessary act
in this ritual surrounding the purchase of a car
when any good American would just head for a bar.
I am almost bitter, limp with relief to see the last
of the Lincoln's taillights disappear around the curve
up the slope of the driveway with this Eastern couple
snug inside, she who clutched a pocketbook to her breast
so like my mother, holding the cashier's check
for the $25,000 while he pulled out $750 in cash and shoved
it at me, so sorry, so sorry, so like my father after a bout
of haggling that leaves me trembling, tears of rage as I say later
what I should've said, I'd drive the Continental over
the retaining wall and run it into a tree to make it worth
his first offer. . . Climbing out of the truck, one foot
rests on the running board, I am closing the door, walking away,
key in hand, I am saying out loud to my father
as if he is walking just ahead of me, I am following
as he strides away, why didn't you know me, I plead
and always the weeping held back each part of each day
pouring out, how could you not know, I shake my fist at my father
who art in Heaven, hallowed be thy name, who would not allow me
to love him while he lived, and I his only child, but my mother,
his first child as well as my older sister who became my baby
lying in the coffin, who would've guessed, not my mother
nor my father, not even myself I never knew before today,
almost everything I'd give away, or sell below cost, but this truck.

EPILOGUE

St. Valentine's Day And The Suicides' Daughter

When you first handed them to me, wrapped in cellophane
          and tied with a red ribbon, I could barely look.
Even the next day as I trimmed the stems and rearranged
          them in a vase, it was as though I saw the red and
cream roses, yellow and pink carnations with one spray
          of fern and baby's breath in sepia, shimmering through
unshed tears like an old photograph, yet each bloom
          so particular and chosen that I would've staked
my life on you only hours before hurling them at your
          half-turned back walking out the door, water
cascading down the slick green Polo jacket I'd bought you
          after you'd blown leaves and pine straw off the roof
of my parents' house where three nineteen year-olds
          who can't quite scrape together the rent each month
now live with three cats and two dogs, a bouquet of fur
          and piss wafting through rooms where my mother,
who could not stand animals in the house, still roams
          in the echo of my father's footsteps, lights
blinking off and on at whim. Just as when we swung
          into the driveway New Year's Eve, you braked,
said, do you see that? They hovered in a bell of smoke
          as we watched while some unfelt unseen wind
blew them up the hill in tandem, as if they are one
          in spirit as never in life, my mother's most
cherished dream, her body lying now in the grave
          beside his where gunpowder may still stain
his fingers; yet how can I know if it was she, or I,
          who pulled the trigger. I take one-third
of the blame, I cried aloud, weeks after the funeral
          inside the cave of my mother's closet, so many
slacks and blouses, skirts, boxes of shoes. But you
          were just a child, Josie said. So were they, I shot
back. Josie, friend, child of my heart, I would not

have lived if she had not directed me then to lie
down on the burgundy carpet in the spot still stained
          with my father's blood so that she could listen
to how I got sideswiped by his legs and arms stretched out
          stiff on the floor forever alone with the sight
of my mother in pink and still as a doll on the bed, so
          much to remember like a tent show at the Southeastern
Fairaganza with midgets and dog men, fat ladies
          with beards, so whacked out myself I don't see
three notes taped to the TV, nor the pink chiffon
          dress and the dark blue suit they wore
at my daughter's wedding laid out on my father's
          bed in the other room, but the silver gun lying
on the floor beside him like my old cap pistol in a red holster
          slung low around the waist of the fringed
skirt of my cowgirl suit, his mouth without teeth yawning
          wide-open as a bedsore, collapsed and dark
as any region of space and time that reflects no light, my eyes
          like stars shooting across the mad angle of his jaw,
dropping down his throat into the Black Hole of his windpipe.
          Your face now an open mouth of slow surprise as I
cannot satisfy the grief of my conclusions, reeling into
          the kitchen, I grab scissors out of the desk drawer
and hurtle after you onto the front deck toward the truck
          you've just bought with a windfall from my mother's
brother's legacy she left me that I gave to you. I rip off
          my robe and clench it under one arm, skim off the white
gown trimmed in royal blue over my head, a gash in the pad
          of my index finger splotching Victoria's Secret
polyester as dull blades gnaw through the nightgown
          you've given me I jerk back into my robe with the pace
of a demon, so that you only get one fake pious glimpse
          of naked white flesh. . . . Never say to me
again that no one could murder two people at once and alone.
          Long before police squeal up the long winding drive
to fill out their forms, before reporters and TV crews

block out family and friends, spittle may froth
at the corners of my mouth, at any moment as I shout out
        Social Security numbers, names and dates, dancing
around the driveway like a boxer pounding my fists
        in the air, I might've bared my fangs and bitten off
a whole handful of an officer's fingers marking their last
        act. Surrounded by his fourteen acres, in love
with his landscaper you say he'd come to love
        as a son, I cannot fuck them back to life,
but I don't doubt my father's passion even when you choose
        a Hallmark money lover's day to say if I really
loved you I'd put half of everything I own in your name.
        $8,000 is nothing, you spit at me in the dark
of midnight, all the piecework I've made of your valentine
        strewn at our feet, the white paint of the new truck
I've smeared and spelled out my name on the left fender
        in the color and shape of a woman's womb. And like
nothing but the housewife you say I've been a lady
        of leisure who reads books, I wipe down the truck
with the same dishrag that washes the sweat and salt tracks
        off my face as I gather the flowers, remnants
of the gown, cradle them in my arms and rock on the floor. . .
        The cardinal's back to beat his beak against
my window this past week, first appearing on a Monday,
        May 21, the third anniversary of my near death
on May 21, three years before three bodies piled up
        in three months

        times 7 is 21, my daughter born on July
                21, reverse the sequence of my son born
        on March 12, your birthday, April 21,
                eight inches of gangrene cut from my small
        intestine, eight inches of a cardinal,
                whirling up and down in a blur of red feathers,
        after my collie, Noah, put down on a Monday,
                April 10, three months before I found my mother

and father on a Monday, July 10, at 7
           in the evening, the cardinal hung around for 7
weeks, and on a Monday, February 10, 1997,
           one year and 7 months later, you come back
for me, two times 7 is 14 acres, 6 + 8 make 14
           letters in your name, 7 + 7 make 14 in mine,

           fourteen days into February, after 7 months we've broken
every taboo, race, age, class, and I know nothing of the stars'
           numerical significance as I knew nothing of my father's
.38 revolver or my mother's final resolve to lie down
           in her brass bed where he pressed the barrel
against her breast and blew a bullethole through her heart.
           Yet I climb into the cab of the idling truck bought
with Mother's money three days after my orgy of mourning
           even though I know I'm the stand-in for your mother
who never says she loves you and never stood up for you
           against the babysitter who made you pee blood
after you said no woman's ever loved you the way I love you,
           I still cringe when you say *molester,* I say *rapist.*
Just as once you plucked the petals off a single rose,
           she loves me, she loves me not scattered across
my driveway, you ply my lips apart to nudge
           yourself in so gently urgent your nail slips
and carves a crescent moon at the mouth on St. Valentine's
           Day, you forget nothing, even the heart-shaped box
bulging with chocolates makes me heavy with your
           craving for a child with red curls and black skin.